34 YEARS IN HELL

MY TIME INSIDE AMERICA'S TOUGHEST PRISONS

JAMIE MORGAN KANE

MIRROR BOOKS

First published by Mirror Books in 2019

Mirror Books is part of Reach plc
10 Lower Thames Street
London EC3R 6EN
England

www.mirrorbooks.co.uk

ISBN 978-1-912624-56-0

Typeset by Danny Lyle
DanJLyle@gmail.com

Printed and bound in Great Britain by
CPI Group (UK) Ltd, Croydon, CR0 4YY

A CIP catalogue record for this book is available from the British Library.

Every reasonable effort has been made to contact all copyright holders, but if there
are any errors or omissions, we will insert the appropriate acknowledgement in
subsequent printings of this book.

1 3 5 7 9 10 8 6 4 2

Cover images: iStockphoto

All other photographs are author's own.

To Betty, who not only believed in me but knew that I was British before I did, and not only proved it, but fought for more than 12 years to get me "home".

And to Matthew, who was always there with encouragement and supported my efforts to get released and return to Britain.

PROLOGUE

Inside the dark cell I was barely able to see, with only a little light coming in through a dirty window covered in mesh and bars. The cell was about six feet wide and eight feet deep, with a stainless steel toilet and sink unit by the door. My bunk was attached to the wall and needed to be unfolded. As I started to lower it, the chains that attached it to the wall rattled loudly and the guy in the other bunk stirred but I wasn't sure if I'd woken him. After I laid out my sheet and blanket on the bunk, I looked out the window. All I could see was a tower along the perimeter fence, with a figure inside it holding a rifle. I laid my head down for the first night of many.

At 5am, the lights came on. My cellmate was dressed and at the door. He gave me a quick glance before the door opened and then he bolted out. I followed him – I was only a moment or two behind him yet he was nowhere to be seen. I queued up behind the other inmates and walked down the stairs and into the chow hall. I picked up a metal tray and was handed a metal fork and spoon. The meal was a surprise – a choice of scrambled, fried or boiled eggs, two strips of bacon, a hamburger patty, a bowl of hot porridge or cold cereal, a cup of mixed fruit, toast, a jelly-filled donut, a cup of orange juice and coffee.

After leaving the serving line I searched for somewhere to sit but noticed people were segregating themselves by race, not something I'd ever done before. Finally one of the guys from my transfer bus called me over to a table and I joined him.

At this time in the California correctional system, there were four groups: White, Black, Hispanic or Other. The others included Native Americans, Pacific Islanders, Asians, those from then Middle or Near East and those of mixed blood. The fact I'd never liked being called white and had the words "Manx Bred" tattooed on my arms caused confusion during my intake, so I'd initially been listed as Other. Eating my meal, I thought at least I wouldn't starve in prison – there had been many times in the county jail when the meals were a bit small. Most of the guys around me were mainly talking about how much time they were doing (a question I was told by older guys in jail never to ask). There was a weird calm in the room, not at all what I was expecting.

After breakfast we returned to our cells. My cellmate wasn't there. Finally, at around 8am, my door opened and I heard, "Wetmore, go down the stairs to the chow hall for orientation." I ended up again with the nine other guys I'd been with last night. A couple of inmates in blue uniforms handed out booklets, pencils, writing paper and envelopes. We were directed to a small section of tables and then in walked one of the biggest men I had ever seen.

This man was about six feet nine inches tall and 300 pounds, and was wearing black-rimmed glasses and carrying a folder. He walked up to the podium in front of us.

"I am Ed Kemper," he said into the microphone in a monotone voice. "It is important to remember – *A man must have a moral compass and one must never deviate from that compass*." He continued to speak though quite honestly I was just wondering who he was, rather than listening to what he had to say.

I was given an answer at dinner. He was none other than Edmund Kemper, a serial killer who had killed 10 people. His first victims were his grandparents when he was a teenager, for which he served six years in a mental facility before the doctors found him sane enough to be released. After his release, he killed six female hitchhikers, and even dismembered and ate parts of them. His mother and her best friend were the final two killings, at which time he turned himself into the police and confessed to all the murders. He had committed most of his crimes in 1972 and 1973 around Santa Cruz in California. As I had been in the US military at that time, I hadn't been aware of his crimes.

When the doctors had cleared him for release over the killing of his grandparents, they said he "lacked confidence and suffered from late puberty". He would later be used as a character type in many books and films, most notably in *The Silence of the Lambs* – Buffalo Bill is based on Ed Kemper. He was also involved in the programme to read books on to tapes for the blind and was said to have recorded about 500 of these – perhaps he did it in that same monotone voice. I have always wondered about Kemper's own "moral compass".

My cellmate returned just before dinner that night but he still hadn't spoken to me. I thought he was sizing me up because of my tattoos, but then heard a soft muffled crying noise coming from his bunk. I said nothing until it had continued for a couple of hours and was keeping me awake.

"Are you all right?" I asked. "Is there anything I can do?"

He sat up in bed. "How can *you* help me do my time?"

I decided to break the one rule I'd been told. "How much time?"

"A year and a day," he said, "but with jail time credits I arrived with 61 days. And I'm now down to 58."

"58 years?"

"No, I said 58 days."

"You've got less than two months to do, and you're crying about it?" I realise this was insensitive but not only would I have welcomed 58 days, but they could have hung me upside down the whole time and I would still have been happy.

"And you? How much time did you get?" he asked.

"27 years to life."

"How will you do that?"

"I'll hold my mud and do the best I can," I replied after a moment's thought.

With that, he rolled over and went to sleep.

My name is Jamie Morgan Kane and for the last 34 years I've been incarcerated in some of America's toughest prisons. Now I'm 65 years old and for the first time in my life I feel free. But what does this freedom mean, when most of my life was based on a lie? For years I believed I was just another citizen of the United States, another soul who had lost their way in the system. But the truth of who I am is so much more complex and unbelievable than I could ever have imagined.

This is the story of my life.

PART 1

1

My very earliest memory is of being in a big house. I was about three or four. The only emotion I can remember is being very scared. I was with my mother and couldn't understand any of the words people were speaking. Suddenly she grabbed me and hid me in a pitch-black cupboard under the stairs. She told me not to move or make a sound. So I stood there, rigid, with her holding me tight, while outside I could hear lots of noise and shouting and what sounded like police whistles blowing. When everything quietened down, my mother took me out of the house into a bitterly cold night. From that moment, the memory fades. It was only years later that I realised why I couldn't understand everyone's words: my mother was Irish and had only taught me to speak Gaelic – I had no understanding of English.

Soon after that, I recall Mother and I travelling on a coach – I was sitting on her lap and we were heading west. The journey seemed endless – we lived and slept on the bus for what seemed like days. I remember passing through countryside with moss hanging from the trees – maybe it was Louisiana or Mississippi. My only other lasting impression was of being constantly hungry, because my mother never had enough money for food.

We reached our destination, a place I later discovered was Phoenix, Arizona, and arrived at the doorstep of a lady who seemed very old to me. My mother seemed to know her, because the lady chastised her the minute she heard me speak.

"Stop him speaking that gibberish," the old lady said.

I'd picked up a few words of English on our journey but still mainly spoke Gaelic. From that day I was taught to speak English properly, although Mother and I still spoke to each other in Gaelic at times. She called this "mummy speak" and often used it when she didn't want other people to understand what we were saying to one another.

I came to know the old lady as Grandma Toby. She would become my best and truest friend until I was 14 years old. She was originally from England and ran a trailer park called The Blue Bonnet. She let Mother and I move into one of the vacant trailers. Although we moved frequently Grandma Toby's park became the closest thing to a home that I would know for years to come.

My mother would often remind me that she was Irish and I wasn't. She would say, "Your Queen is Elizabeth and your

King is Manannan." I had no idea what she meant, but I always understood that I was different – different from the other children and different from her. I learned that King Manannan is a Celtic god of the sea who is thought to be the protector of the Isle of Man. Mother was always fond of Celtic myths and legends and told them endlessly, though I never once saw her reading a story from a book. It was her knowledge that generated my love and study of Celtic history when I grew older.

I'd heard Mother use many other names for herself but she never stopped telling me, "Always remember that your mother's real name is Moya Iris Kane, and that you're called Jamie."

My most enduring memory of her was as a young, bouncy and beautiful woman, who laughed and played with me a lot. She would take me to Encanto Park in Phoenix, where she used to skip and dance barefoot in the park – just like in the film starring Robert Redford and Jane Fonda. As the day drew to a close, we would sit on the grass. Looking at the dusk sky she would tell me she was from Baile Bhuirne in County Cork, in Ireland.

"My family was originally from Derry, but due to the politics in the North my father moved the family to Cork before I was born," she would say.

I always felt like she longed to be back in her home town.

Mother told me I'd been born in Hillberry on the Isle of Man in a home birth that had taken 14 long and painful hours. She said my birth hadn't been formally registered but that I was baptised on 27 February 1954, the day she always celebrated as my birthday. She used 27 February as her birthday too, as she said she hadn't started to live until she saw and held me for the first time, so we celebrated together. Mother impressed upon me that my full name was Morgan James Kane. Although she always called me Jamie there were odd times when we were speaking Gaelic to each other, that she would call me "Murghey". There were also times when she would repeat *"Remember, remember, remember,"* when she was telling me something she thought I should know. On one of these occasions she told me, "You are a *Man of the Isle, Son of the Sea, Brother of the Storm.*" I felt this was of such importance that as an adult I even had these words tattooed across my neck line. Interestingly though, she never taught any Gaelic to the daughters she later had. My belief now, knowing my true history, is that my inability to speak English was a deliberate ploy to prevent anyone from understanding me in case I tried to express any memories of my very early life.

I never felt comfortable asking my mother about my father, but finally one day I did. She told me he was also Manx and was a lovely, kind and generous man, but she never told me his name. Throughout our time together I never heard her say

4

one bad word about him – no matter how many hardships we went through. Hard times were never far away, and we often struggled to feed ourselves. To avoid paying rent, we would do a "moonlight flit". On many occasions we had no place to sleep so Mother would find an unlocked car and we would creep on to the back seat and sleep there, always leaving just before dawn. I must have been only five years old but even then I knew from very early on that she and my father hadn't been married, and she didn't wear a wedding ring.

"When you were just a baby, we left by ship for Canada," she told me. "You were such a good baby on the journey. You didn't cry – not once."

I had so many questions for her but didn't want to interrupt her story, as it was so rare for her to tell me things about my past. "Of course once we got to Canada, things didn't work out with the family so that's why we kept moving. And that's why we're here in the United States."

2

The early part of my life was chaotic. I was never sent to school. Instead I spent many of my days either alone in a cheap motel room waiting for my mother to return, or out playing in a local canal catching crayfish. Mother gave me the impression that I was somehow a secret and that I shouldn't talk to strangers. When we were out, if we ever saw a priest or a nun walking towards us we would quickly cross over the road or step into a store to avoid them, although she never explained why. My friends were mainly the children of the migrant workers who came to stay at Grandma Toby's trailer park for short periods while their parents worked in the fields.

One day without warning, we moved to Phoenix. My mother met and quickly married a man called Butterfield who was big and smelly with a dirty green truck. He moved us into his house and for the first time ever I experienced what living in a house was like. Sadly, the marriage was a very violent one. Her husband often beat her.

One time, even though I was only little, I tried to save my mother while Butterfield was attacking her. He picked me up and threw me against the wall, badly bruising me. Mother rushed at him to save me from further harm and scratched his face. He hit her a few more times then walked out of the house, never to return. I still have a vivid memory of her sitting in a bath of bloody water with me beside her crying bitterly because she was so hurt. Somehow I felt it was all my fault.

Now Mother no longer had a husband or money, we found ourselves back at Grandma Toby's trailer park. Soon after she gave birth to a daughter, Janet, and then Janet, Mother and I were on the road again. This time we moved into various motels where Mother worked as a cleaner to pay our rent. While she was working, Janet and I would be left alone in our room. I doubt I did a very good job of looking after the baby because all we had to eat was bread smeared with butter and sprinkled with sugar. But I did learn how to change a nappy, which I was proud of.

Just before my sixth birthday my mother married another man, Daniel Kearns. He lived in Los Angeles and we moved there. I don't know where Mother disappeared off to next but she left us with the Kearns family. They didn't treat me and Janet well, and we hoped Mother would come back soon. Fortunately she did return, carrying a small bundle – another baby daughter she called Pamala.

One day I upset Daniel's brother, who also lived with us. He was frequently drunk and I often saw him beat my mother. Daniel was too afraid to intervene, so I collected his brother's whisky bottles from around the house and emptied them. Of course this made Daniel's brother even more angry, so he took off his thick leather belt and started whipping me hard. The firm leather made a loud sound each time it struck me – nearly as painful as the feeling itself. I ran out of the house to get away from him but fell to the ground. He caught up and started lashing out at me again as I lay there, exhausted and helpless. For the second time in my life, my mother threw herself on me to protect me and, as before, she was badly hurt.

The next thing I knew, I was all alone with a label pinned to my coat, on a long-distance bus back to Phoenix. Despite the journey taking around eight hours, I only had a bag of sweets. Fortunately for me, an older woman took pity on me and shared her food. Once we arrived at the Greyhound bus station, the woman phoned the number written on my label and I was collected by a man who took me back to Grandma Toby's.

I was with Grandma Toby for a few months before Mother and Daniel showed up to take me back to Los Angeles. While I was happy for us all to be back together again, deep down I had a feeling it wouldn't last. And I was right. After yet another explosive argument, we headed back to Phoenix.

Mother took us back to Grandma Toby's, expecting to leave us all there yet again. But it didn't happen that way.

"I don't know what you thought you were going to do, but only the boy can stay," was what I heard. I've spent years trying to understand what the old lady meant, but her next words echo in my memory to this day. "He is mine – they are not," she said holding me in front of her. With nothing more than a shrug Mother walked away with the girls, leaving me there for almost a year.

During that time, Grandma Toby's friend Earl, the man who had picked me up from the bus station, took an interest in me. He took me to hardware stores and taught me about mechanical things. He was always dressed for manual work and I can still see him in his freshly ironed but heavily stained overalls at the start of each day. He taught me how to fit pipes together and how to repair washing machines and electric fans. At weekends he would take me to the Gila and Verde rivers, where he taught me how to skip stones and float down them in an inner tube. His wife Doris used to make the most wonderful pies – I particularly liked her peach cobbler. He was my first positive male role model and I remember our time together fondly.

For the next nine years, I spent a lot of time with Grandma Toby. I had the most fun when I stayed with her. She had a little house in one corner of the trailer park and let me sleep on her living room floor. She fed me well – I was never cold or hungry – and even bought me new clothes. Some days, Earl and Doris would drive us all out to picnics at South Mountain. Earl had a little hexagonal squeeze box with pearl buttons which he would take out and play on these trips.

I didn't see Mother again until she turned up with Pamala and yet another new baby, who she introduced as Tricia. Janet was nowhere to be seen – I was led to believe that Mother had returned her to her father, Mr Butterfield. Just like every other time Mother had shown up on Grandma Toby's doorstep, I had to pack my belongings and leave the only loving home I'd known, only for her to abandon us at our next destination. This time she left us with some strangers in a house in Cashion, just west of Phoenix. There seemed to be several other children there all about the same ages, so I think they must have been watching children for other people as well. We all slept on the floor in the garage with dirty burlap sacks for blankets.

When Mother came to get me the next time, she was without Pamala and Tricia. She told me she'd left them with their father in Los Angeles so it was just Mother and me on our own, like before. I never really knew if she cared for me or not, but she did worry about me. I remember making friends with a boy who lived near us. One day he invited me to come with him to earn some money painting house numbers on kerbs. We left before dawn while Mother was still sleeping, because we had to walk a great distance to the neighbourhoods where the better-off people lived. I pulled the little wagon that contained the paint, stencils and brushes, while he knocked on doors to see if anyone wanted anything painted and also collected the money. We gave people a choice between a black background with white letters or a white background with black letters. We charged 50 cents and he gave me half. This left me with so much change that I had to remove a sock to put it all in.

It was well after dark by the time I arrived home. Mother screamed out, "Morgan James Kane, where have you been?" She grabbed me and shook me, holding me close to her while crying. When she had calmed down, I handed her my sockful of change and said, "Here, Mother. I was trying to earn some money so you don't have to work so hard."

She started crying again. "Don't ever do that again," she said. "I was so worried about you, I thought something might have happened to you. Promise you will never, ever go out without telling me."

"I promise," I said, relieved that she cared.

But once again, just as many times before, she would leave me.

3

As the years passed, Mother left me with greater frequency. She would disappear for days at a time, sometimes without warning. She would leave in the middle of the night and I would wake to discover she was gone. If we were living in a motel at the time, she would leave me with a pile of comics or colouring books and tell me to keep quiet, and also what to do when someone knocked on the door.

"You wait for a few moments, then open the door and you'll find a plate of food waiting for you outside," she told me. "You make sure you eat all of it. And when you're done, put the plate back outside the door and shut the door again, but never leave this room. OK?"

This occurred on more than a dozen occasions.

I didn't attend a formal school until I was about 14, but I was taught how to read, write and do sums by Grandma Toby. Once, when Mother left me with a family on the San Carlos

Apache Reservation, the kids there taught me how to find water in the desert and which plants were edible. They also taught me how to start a fire and make moccasins, as well as other basic Native American survival skills. That family gave me the nickname "Sunrise", because the old grandma there said that my hair's reddish tint, my smile and my blue eyes reminded her of the sky in the early morning. One of my favourite memories of that time was when a tribal police officer who used to ride a big Appaloosa horse would toss candies to us as we scrambled to catch them.

Instead of going to school, Mother would take me to work with her when she was around. I remember travelling east out of Phoenix along Van Buren Street, where she worked as a domestic in wealthy people's houses in Paradise Valley, Scottsdale or Tempe. I looked forward to going with her mainly because I'd often be fed there, and a good meal was hard to come by at that point. If I could, I would try to hide some of the food so I could take it home.

Given how little we used to eat and the uncertainty of where our next meal was coming from it wasn't surprising that I developed a thyroid problem. It was Grandma Toby who spotted that something wasn't right. She noticed my eyes were bulging out and realised I wasn't gaining weight and was becoming hyperactive. She took me to the doctor, who diagnosed Graves' Disease. Unfortunately, because Grandma Toby wasn't my legal guardian the doctor wouldn't prescribe any treatment for me. When Grandma Toby told Mother about the doctor Mother ignored her, perhaps because we had no extra money for medical bills.

Mother was changing: she was no longer the carefree woman who'd leave in the middle of the night and tell me stories from my past. Being an obedient child, I accepted that I should do what I was told so didn't ever question anything about my life. But the hard reality was that Mother was frequently drunk and I had to watch over her, cleaning her up when she was sick and even sometimes bathing her and sitting beside her to make sure she didn't pass out in the tub. There was another change too: she would often bring various male friends home with her, but I shut my eyes and ears to what was going on. I had to do as I was told and stay out of sight. I never understood why I couldn't be like the other kids. One day when I asked her, she snapped and shouted, "Because you're in the United States illegally and we would get into trouble if anyone found out. They would find us and separate us. Do you want that to happen?"

Then one day, something felt very different. Mother took Grandma Toby aside and spoke to her privately. I couldn't hear anything because their voices were really low but I could see that Grandma Toby was crying. As we turned to go out the door, Grandma Toby cried out, "Wait a minute, wait a minute, I've got something for him." She went into her bedroom and came out carrying a small velvet-covered box, which she handed to me. I opened this curious box slowly, to find what looked like a silver gentleman's pocket watch inside. It had a braided cord that looked like it was made out of hair, and halfway down the cord hung a gold lion's head. Inside the lid of the watch was a beautiful picture of a young Grandma Toby. It was certainly a very impressive piece of jewellery. As she gave it to me her voice slightly cracking, she simply said, "All fine young gentlemen carry a good timepiece." That was the last time I ever saw Grandma Toby.

Within a few days, Mother dressed me up in really smart clothes I'd never seen before and told me we were going out. At the time we were living in a motel somewhere in Phoenix. It was a really hot day, sticky and humid. As we walked down the street she held my hand more tightly than usual. I was now 14, but was small for my age because of my thyroid problem, so I kind of liked this extra attention from her.

She remained silent as we walked towards the bus stop. It was only when we were sitting on the bus that she said, "It will be all right." I didn't know what would be all right – was she talking about the ride or the day? It seemed just like any other time we'd rode the bus downtown, except for the fancy clothes I was wearing. After around 45 minutes she said, "Let's go, this is our stop."

We got off the bus and turned east, heading down the street passing stores with big display windows. Normally we would stop and linger, looking at all the things we could never have, but not that day. It was different – there was an almost hurried feeling as she began pulling me along. I'd never known Mother to be in such a hurry before.

Once we had walked a few blocks, we stopped. She turned and looked at me and said very softly in almost a whisper, "Promise me you'll be a good boy." She smoothed out her dress and straightened my shirt. Then, using her spit on a handkerchief, matted down my cowlick and cleaned off any imaginary dirt that she thought was on my face.

We crossed the road and entered the Carnation Ice Cream Parlour. It was cool inside and smelled wonderful. A couple rose from a nearby booth, came over to us and introduced themselves.

"Hello young man – I am Charles Wetmore and this is my wife Alice."

The man made a comment about how small I was for my age and how I looked underfed, but the woman just gave me a big hug. Then she took me over to the counter while Mr Wetmore and Mother sat in a booth. The woman told the counter girl to get me anything I wanted and told me to stay sitting there because the grown-ups needed to talk. After looking at the menu I ordered a lime freeze because it looked so good in the picture. I started eating it. After around 15 minutes, Mother and the Wetmores walked over to me. Mother kissed my cheek and combed over my cowlick again while saying, "I'll be going away for a little while, so you'll stay with these nice people. Be good for them, and I'll see you soon."

I watched her walk out the door for what was the last time I would ever see her. Mr Wetmore was holding the small case that Mother had brought with us that morning, which I later found out contained clothes for me. He gave me a rough nudge off the stool and said it was time to go home. Walking out of the ice cream parlour, my life changed forever, and I've never cared for the taste of lime ever since.

4

I had a strange feeling I'd seen this couple somewhere before. As we got into their car I wondered if my mother may have worked for them at various times over three or four years, cleaning or as a waitress at dinner parties. She worked in a lot of houses but all her jobs were sporadic.

From that day on, I had to learn that my name was now John Raymond Wetmore, and that I should answer to John. My year of birth was now 1956 rather than 1954. My new parents' names were Charles Henry and Alice Elizabeth Wetmore, and I had to memorise their address even though I was never allowed out of the house. When any visitor came to the front door I was sent to my bedroom so that nobody could see me.

I wasn't the only child in the house: there was a little girl called Susan who was around seven years younger than me. She was also adopted. For as long as I lived with the Wetmores, I never managed to get close to Susan. She always seemed to be wary of me for some reason. Certainly when I first came to live with them she kept repeating the haunting words, "You're not my John. You're the wrong John."

Mrs Wetmore bought me a wardrobe of brand new clothes. I'd never had so many in my life. Strangely there was already a great deal of boy's clothing in the house, but it was all a bit too small for me to wear. So Mrs Wetmore called a local charity and arranged for them to collect it. Mr Wetmore came home at the same moment as the big yellow truck was parking outside the house. That was the first time I saw him lose his temper. He yelled so loud when he saw the truck that I could hear him from inside, and it caused the neighbours to come out to see what was going on.

Sadly, it wasn't the last time he would get mad.

Not long after that incident, everything in the house was packed up in large boxes and transferred into a removal van. That night Dr Wetmore went to sleep in a hotel.

"I can't possibly sleep on the floor but you and the kids have to stay here Alice," he said. "And anyways, *he* can't be seen outside the house." He pointed his finger sharply at me.

So Mrs Wetmore, Susan and I slept in the empty, cold house on the bare wooden floor with only a pile of blankets to keep us warm. When Dr Wetmore returned in the morning he brought some fast food burgers and sodas for breakfast. Before we left, he asked our neighbour to take a photo of the four of us standing in front of the house, smiling. I don't have many photos of me when I was young but I still have a copy of this one – it's the only one of me as a little boy with what looked like a real family.

We drove from Arizona to Fresno in California. I was told the move was because Dr Wetmore had finished his doctorate degree at Arizona State University and was taking up a teaching position in the business school at the university in Fresno. Our new home meant new rules, which I didn't particularly like. But as soon as he'd given me yet another order he casually told me that he'd given my mother $10,000 for me, that I was adopted and crucially, he now owned me. He insisted I pretend I was 12. I didn't feel comfortable doing this but if I objected he threatened to harm my mother if I told anyone my true name and age. It wasn't long before his verbal threats became physical violence, especially when I refused to follow his orders.

I was taken to see a paediatrician in Fresno. After an examination she told me that I needed my tonsils removed, but she assured me that I could have all the ice cream I wanted after my surgery. Of course I agreed – what kid would refuse ice cream? But when I came round from the anaesthetic I found I still had my tonsils and had been circumcised instead. I can feel my pain and confusion to this day. Apparently Dr Wetmore had pre-arranged this with the doctor. I've always wondered whether it was ethical for a doctor to tell a patient one thing and then perform a different, unnecessary operation.

"Why did you do this to me?" I asked Dr Wetmore when I was released from the hospital.

"Because properly groomed people are not uncircumcised," he replied, without a second's thought.

In the autumn of 1968 Dr Wetmore said to me, "Now you listen John, if anyone asks, you tell them you were schooled in Arizona. Do you hear that?" Again he threatened to harm my mother if I told the truth. He registered me at Ahwahnee Middle School, Fresno, my first-ever school. I was supposed to go into seventh grade but when I was tested, thanks to the school of Grandma Toby, my scores were so high that they decided to let me skip two grades and I was put in ninth grade instead. I was happy to just have the opportunity to go to school in the first place – that was one lie I could live with.

Every Sunday Dr Wetmore would make us attend church. I always found this to be at odds with his character because in all the years of living with him, he never behaved like a Christian in any way, shape or form. I think church for him was an opportunity to "see, and be seen". Frequently after church we would go out for brunch and then visit model home showings or shopping malls, where he would disappear off and have private meetings with his associates. Neither Mrs Wetmore, Susan or I could eavesdrop on these meetings – we could only observe him from a distance.

Dr Wetmore was a fairly tall man, about five feet eleven inches. He liked to put on airs that made him seem like he came from a well-to-do, aristocratic family. He drummed into me that I was Irish scum and I wasn't anywhere near as good as he was. What he wanted was somebody very subservient who would obey and bow down to his every word. He'd already accomplished this with Mrs Wetmore and Susan but I, on the other hand, was a tougher challenge.

I decided very early on that I was never going to give in or be broken by him. I was nobody's slave. This would often lead to big disagreements, and I would challenge almost everything he asked of me. So he beat me – because I was small but also because I scared him, I think. Yet no matter how badly he beat me, I wouldn't cry. He'd have this disarming look in his eyes. The longer I didn't cry, the harder he would beat me, until eventually he would give up. He wasn't used to that because even adults were afraid of him and would do whatever he wanted – it wasn't unusual for him to boast about how he could ruin people.

By the spring of 1969, the beatings were a daily occurrence. One time during a beating I fell down hard. Normally this would be enough for him to stop but this time he started kicking me. I can't remember what started it, but I know that he was beating me in the back yard by a tree. He'd normally put my arms around the tree while he beat my back and legs with a thick razor strop. Somehow I found myself on the ground. He was beating and kicking me so hard that I had to be rushed to the hospital emergency room with a ruptured appendix.

"No matter what he says, he's lying," I overheard him tell the doctor. "He was roughhousing with some other boys I'd told him not to be around, and they hurt him." I was just thankful to be alive.

This abuse carried on for about four years, but while the severity of his physical attacks lessened as I got older, the verbal and mental abuse continued. Though he did abuse Mrs Wetmore verbally, I never saw him get physical with her or Susan.

I found out that a number of women in Mrs Wetmore's family had died of cancer so she'd had a double mastectomy in her teens, which is why they decided to adopt rather than have their own children. She did have days when she couldn't do much and I would try to help all I could, just as I'd done for my own mother. We tried to help each other but the reality of life with Dr Wetmore was about to become even harder to deal with, although I didn't realise it could get any worse at the time.

5

At the start of the new school year I transferred from Ahwahnee Middle School to Hoover High. I'd been attending high school for a year. I especially liked science and was really into mechanics and anything I could fix with my hands. I felt useful, which is probably why I liked it so much. I did OK in math – as I only had to know up to pre-algebra to graduate, I was fine with just getting by. All in all, I guess you could say that my studies went well. I was into a few sports too, including cross-country running. I may have had short legs, but I had great endurance.

My real joy though came from building things. So that year I decided to buy a car and made sure I learnt to drive. I desperately wanted a 1956 Chevy Bel Air. Mrs Wetmore didn't drive and we only had Dr Wetmore's 1967 Plymouth Fury III, which he used every day for his business. As Dr Wetmore insisted I was 14 (even though I was really 16), he said he would list himself as the legal owner but I could have the car if I paid for it myself, as well as for all the licensing, registration fees and maintenance costs. Of course he would keep hold of the car keys, but if that's what it took to get my own car then I was going to do it. I started off by mowing neighbours' lawns, washing cars, walking dogs and doing chores around the house for Mrs Wetmore – and before not too long I was able to earn the money needed to buy the car and pay for its running expenses.

Dr and Mrs Wetmore signed for me to get a special permit to drive as long as there was an adult in the car. I was all set. I'd seen an advertisement on a bulletin board at the market from a guy who was selling two cars for $500 each. I noted down the number and made arrangements to visit him at the first opportunity.

Mrs Wetmore kindly came to the bank to help me take the money out from my account. I had $500 in my hand and she suddenly pulled out another $50.

"Just in case," she said.

A friend's father and brother drove me and two of my friends to see the cars. The first was a 1967 Pontiac LeMans, with a 326 cubic inch motor, wide tyres in the back and a "gunslinger pistol" shifter. It was green with a black vinyl top. Everyone thought this was the one I should buy, but it was the second car that did it for me. It didn't run – the motor was out and sitting in the boot – though all the new parts to rebuild it were there. This was the 1956 Chevy Bel

Air two-door hardtop in original condition that I'd been dreaming about. From the eagle on the bonnet to the rear fins, it was a real beauty.

"She's beautiful, isn't she?" said the guy selling it. "I got her from the factory with a 1956 Corvette, 265 cubic inch motor with a six pack carb set up." Then, with a smile he added, "Once this baby gets back together she'll smoke most other cars around."

That's all he needed to say – I'd heard enough, my mind was made up.

Once I paid him for the Chevy the main problem was how to drag a car in bits and parts all the way back home. My friend's dad called the auto shop teacher at Hoover High and explained the situation. It was agreed that if I could get the car to the school, I could store it in one of the work bays. The teacher would meet us there and let us in. That's when I remembered I still had the extra $50 in my pocket, which I decided I was going to share with my friends. We would push the car ourselves, me steering and my two friends pushing, all the way to school.

I couldn't wait for auto shop classes to start. I was elated that I, along with my school friends, would be putting together something from scratch. Also, I was pleased I didn't have to share it with anyone and I felt hugely proud that I was able to do this. We made sure to start with the harder work: putting the parts together, wiring the car and rebuilding the engine. When all this was done, we had the fun job of painting the bodywork. It was all starting to come together. With each day I could see the beauty I'd imagined when I first bought the car. And all at no extra cost for labour.

I really thought I'd aced the project but it turned out that my differences of opinion with the way the teacher taught the course meant that he gave me a B. I wasn't too fond of his habit of showing us both the right and the wrong ways to work on the car – it just didn't make sense to me. Surely we only needed to know the right – proper – way to work on a vehicle.

I didn't really care that he gave me a low mark though, as I'd spent just $750 for what many considered to be one of the coolest cars at the school. I'd drive it to school and park it in the students' parking lot so that my friends and I could hang out together. It used to upset Dr Wetmore that I felt the need to drive my car to school when we lived right across the street, but I didn't care. And nor did I care that the teacher stopped me from signing up for his class in the following semester. That was one of the finest summers I'd ever had.

Now that I couldn't attend auto shop class I didn't have many choices – I was left with swimming or home economics. Well, I sure as hell wasn't going to take up swimming as it was the middle of winter and swimming in an unheated pool wasn't my idea of fun. That left me with home economics, where I was going to learn about sewing and cooking. This turned out to have additional benefits besides teaching practical life skills, as it also happened to be a class full of girls. I was the only boy in the class, so I had lots of girls wanting to help me all the time. What initially brought all sorts of ribbing from my friends quickly turned on them; it must have been a big surprise for the home economics teacher when more than a dozen other guys signed up to take the class in the next trimester.

The auto shop teacher wasn't the only one I had trouble with. My teachers in history and English were just as tough to learn from. What I knew of the world I'd learned from Grandma Toby, who had taught me about European and English cultures. The history teacher only seemed to know history from an American point of view: how it had always been America that "saved the day" and how they were smarter than every other country in the world. I would point out flaws in some of his teaching, so eventually he would never call on me in class or allow me to read any papers out loud, as others could.

With the English teacher it was much simpler — the problem was that Grandma Toby had taught me to spell words the "English" way. For example, "honour" not "honor", "colour" not "color" and so on, but it meant I lost credit on my papers. I did take it up with my counsellor who made sure my scores were recognised, but the teacher and I never quite saw eye to eye as she would say, "This is America, not England."

By the time I was actually 18, which by Dr Wetmore's insistence was technically 16, I was graduating. I told my school counsellor that there was a mistake on my birth year, to which he simply said, "Oh, OK," and changed it. It was that simple. It had been the policy during the late 1960s of the Vietnam War that when a boy turned 17 and a half, the school would start the procedure of registering them for Selective Service (or what was known as the draft). It allowed the US government to have a pool of young men they could call up for military service.

As I hadn't been registered my number couldn't be called, but the school counsellor went directly to Dr Wetmore citing that the "minor error in my school records" had been corrected and that I would also be signed up for Selective Service. For whatever reason Dr Wetmore contacted a congressional friend of his, Mr Barry Goldwater Jr, and somehow arranged an appointment for me at the Air Force Academy. I didn't know this for a good couple of weeks before it happened. Even then I only found out because Susan, being the typical bratty little sister, came into my room boasting she had a secret.

Susan would often overhear things when I wasn't around and then tell me what she'd heard. But there was always a price on what she knew. She usually wanted a toy or candy if I wanted to know certain pieces of information that she thought could be useful to me. Most times I didn't fall for her blackmail tactics but this time something in the way she said, "You really want to know" made me take notice. So after I went and got her some candy from the store she told me that some important friends of Daddy's were coming to see me the following week and that I would be in the US Air Force, just as he had been. I wasn't sure what Dr Wetmore had planned but as I had constantly refused to bend to his will, I was determined this would be no exception.

The next day at school the counsellor planned to take a number of us boys down to the military recruitment offices. As I was now on record as being 18, I didn't need parental permission to enlist. I told the counsellor that I would like to be put on the list with the other boys. He was pleased and congratulated me on my patriotism, which made me feel proud. Years later I found out that schools got extra money from the federal government for each boy they got to enlist, which is probably why the counsellor took the boys to the recruitment centres during school hours.

I didn't say a word to anyone, not even to the friends I would be going with. When we arrived there were recruiters from the army, navy and marines, but the air force office was closed, which disappointed a few in our group. The navy and the marines shared the same office but were on different sides of the room. A few of my friends went to talk to the marine recruiter, but to be quite honest I didn't think I was "tough enough" to be a marine – and besides, the navy seemed to be as far away from the air force as possible.

"Why do you keep looking at them, boy?" the recruiter snapped at me during our discussion pointing at my friends who were gathered around one table.

"I'm hoping I go with them Sir, but I really don't want to kill anyone," I answered, trying hard not to sound too weak so he wouldn't pick me at all.

His eyes lit up. "Have I got the job for you." He proceeded to tell me about being a hospital corpsman. "So I see you put down mechanics as your hobby on your application. Well, this is just like being a mechanic, except instead of fixing machines you get to fix people. And as a corpsman you'll serve with the marines if you want to but navy is where the smarter people go." And with that, he turned and gave me a wink.

So I signed up to become a corpsman there and then. And more importantly, I got to stay with my friends.

It was hard to keep this secret. I hoped the counsellor wouldn't say anything to Dr Wetmore as I wanted to spring my surprise on him at the right time. Well the right time came the following Friday. I drove home from school to find I couldn't park anywhere in front of the house. There were already a number of large black cars outside, some with drivers leaning on them as I walked past. I made sure I carried my enlistment papers with me every day so they couldn't be accidentally found. As I walked up the drive towards the house, I patted my jacket to reassure myself that the papers were in my pocket before I went in. I'd barely made it across the doorway when Mrs Wetmore ushered me into Dr Wetmore's study, somewhere I wasn't normally allowed.

Once inside, I found about a dozen men standing around with cigarettes and drinks in their hands. They all turned to face me and for the first time I saw what appeared to be a smile on Dr Wetmore's face.

"I got a surprise for you!" he said.

Mr Goldwater Jr a congressman, handed me a rolled-up document with a gold ribbon tied around it. As he did this, the other men in the room moved aside to reveal a large cake on the table. I stepped forward to take a look at the cake which was decorated with the outline of the Air Force Academy and perfect icing saying, "Off we go into the Wild Blue Yonder."

"Congratulations son, this is your appointment to the Academy," Mr Goldwater Jr said, extending his hand towards me.

I turned to Dr Wetmore.

"Oh, Father, here is something for you," I said as I handed him my own enlistment papers.

There was a moment of silence. Dr Wetmore tried to make sense of the papers while the other men just looked on in shock. Then in a flash he hit me across the mouth with such force that I was knocked to the floor. He turned and flipped the cake so high in the air that Mrs Wetmore was still cleaning some of it off the ceiling the next day.

"Go to your room now you ungrateful bastard. I'll deal with you later," he yelled. I did as he said, but with a satisfied smile that he couldn't see.

After everyone had left Mrs Wetmore came up to my room. "What you just did there young man, is unforgivable," she said. "Charles pulled in a lot of favours from his influential friends. He is never going to forgive you for embarrassing him like that. This time you've gone too far – he worked so hard to get you that placement. I really thought this would bring you closer, that maybe it would be the thing that brought you together as father and son. How wrong was I?"

At that moment I felt a surge of guilt for letting her down and for how I handled the situation but I didn't regret signing up on my own. For the next couple of months Dr Wetmore didn't speak a word to me. Instead he asked his wife to relay things to me while giving me some very hateful looks.

After that incident Dr Wetmore seemed to take a lot more business trips than usual, including one notable visit to his friend Richard M. Nixon, President of the United States, who was suddenly under investigation for Watergate. Dr Wetmore seemed to know a lot of people in high places. Apparently he and President Nixon had been friends since the 1950s and Dr Wetmore had supported both of his bids to become president.

I often wondered whether his friendship with President Nixon and other high-ranking politicians was the reason I found myself in the situation that would change my life forever.

I couldn't wait for the first day of August to arrive as this was when I would go to "boot camp". It wasn't just that it would be an adventure — I would finally be away from that house and away from him. I believed he couldn't hurt me any more, though I would very soon find out just how wrong I was.

6

On 1 August 1972, I joined the US Navy. About 30 of us were driven to Fresno Airport by the recruiters and put on planes to take us to our boot camps in San Diego, California. Our new adventure would start from here.

On arrival there were two buses waiting for us – one for those going to the marines training and the other for the navy. I said goodbye to my friends who were getting on the other bus, as large men yelled at us all to "stow our gear and get our asses on board".

Our bus finally stopped in a parking lot in the middle of a number of two-storey buildings, all painted grey ("Battleship Grey", I would soon learn). A man wearing a uniform came on to the bus and started to tell us what to do.

"Leave all contraband on the bus," he shouted at us in a gruff tone. "That means any alcohol, pornography, food and weapons. You will pick up your bag from outside the bus and find a spot on the tarmac and, placing your bag behind you,

you are to stand at attention until told different." He took a breath and, stepping off the bus yelled, "Get you asses in gear and move out!"

So along with all the other guys I quickly got off and looked for my bag. Once found, I headed for the tarmac, where there were coloured circles painted on the ground. We each stood on a coloured circle, placed our bag behind us as we'd been instructed and stood up as straight and tall as we could. Looking up at the sign above me, I read "Welcome to Worm Island".

We probably stood there for about half an hour and still no one came out to speak to us. The bus had driven away and a number of the guys were beginning to get antsy and didn't want to keep standing still. Finally a naval officer and two other staff members came out of the building in front of us and stepped on to the little podium we were facing. After tapping the microphone a couple of times to check it was working, he began, "Congratulations on becoming members of the United States Navy." He was just about to say something else when another bus pulled up and unloaded four guys in handcuffs. These guys were escorted to spots behind us before their cuffs were taken off. The bus driver then handed an envelope to the officer before getting back on the bus and driving away.

"Well, now that we're all in attendance, I can get on with my welcoming speech," the officer continued. "For the next few days, you will be getting processed before being placed in your recruit companies. This process will consist of medical, physical, psychological and swim testing. I expect you all to give 100 percent effort in all that is requested of you and I hope that by the time your eight weeks of boot camp are up, the majority of you will graduate and go on to serve with distinction in the United States Navy." He then introduced the two men who had escorted him. They were both first class petty officers in charge of our recruit company. "I want you to know that there will be additional recruits to our companies arriving throughout the night, so don't expect much sleep," he said. "Goodnight and God bless, gentlemen." And then he stepped down from the podium.

Once the officer had left, the two petty officers took over and instructed us to open our bags and remove any contraband we had with us.

"This is your last chance to avoid any disciplinary," one of them said.

They walked around and bagged up everything that had been cast aside. They also conducted a quick search of our bags. One of the petty officers removed a loaf of bread from the bag of the guy standing next to me.

"Didn't you hear?" the petty officer asked, getting right up in this guy's face. "No weapons are allowed to be brought on to this base without authorisation."

"But sir, it's just bread that my mom baked for me."

The petty officer banged the loaf against the ground half a dozen times, causing it to break. "You could have killed somebody with that," he told the guy, turning to face the rest of us.

The last comment did raise quite a bit of laughter, which didn't go down well with the petty officer, who started screaming at us to stand at attention.

"You are each going to hear your names called out," he shouted. "When you do so, collect your bag and form a line up in front of the officer who called you. They will lead you to your designated barracks."

The petty officer who called my name was a gunner's mate, first class. "I expect perfection from each and everyone one of you lot – even the most flawed ones," he said. "Now follow me."

We did as he asked but our marching manner was somewhat sloppy. Once we reached our barracks we grabbed whichever bunk we wanted and settled in. This would be our home for the next eight weeks. Our officer pointed to the brooms and mops inside the front door and explained that we had to make our barracks ship-shape before making our bunks and being allowed to go to bed.

"I'll be sending somebody around to check," he said.

So we started cleaning. It took us a couple of hours to get the barracks ready – it sure did seem that someone had purposely made a mess for us to clean up. Just as we finished and were putting the cleaning gear back where we found it, in came a second-class petty officer who told us we had exactly five minutes to make our bunks before lights out. It was around 1am.

I don't know how long I slept but I was woken suddenly by the sound of metal trash cans being beaten and the lights being turned on.

"Get up, get up, get up. You've got 90 seconds to be dressed and on the tarmac. Find yourself a circle."

I quickly pulled on my clothes and shoes, and ran out of the barracks into pitch darkness along with the rest of the guys. We still hadn't finished dressing by the time we hit the tarmac, and all I could hear was yelling from our barracks at the guys who were still half-asleep. We were joined by another group of guys from a separate barracks.

"Gentlemen, it is now 3.30am and it's time for chow. I suggest you eat well – you have a long day ahead of you.'

The chow hall was on the other side of the buildings.

"Grab one tray, one set of silverware, one cup and head down the line," several sailors instructed us. "Place your tray in front of each server and take whatever they have in front of them."

The first thing served was toast with chipped beef gravy on it – which is more commonly known as "shit on a shingle" – followed by scrambled eggs, a slice of ham, two pieces of fruit, a donut and a bowl of oatmeal. At the very end of the line, we were given hot black coffee and a carton of milk. We were directed to a set of tables near the exit door, given five minutes to eat our meal and told not to leave anything on the tray.

Before I could finish my coffee a whistle sounded and we filed out. We crossed paths with smiling sailors. We were still in our civvies and, more crucially, most of us still had long hair. Little did we know that our next stop was the barber shop, where there were six chairs waiting for us, with six barbers standing behind them. There was a hippy recruit sitting in a chair a couple down from me. His barber asked him if he would like to keep his sideburns.

The guy answered all too eagerly, "Yes please, it's taken me a few years to grow them out!"

The barber removed both of the sideburns with his clippers, placed them in a plastic bag and handed them over. This guy was so shocked that for the full eight weeks in boot camp he would still talk about the incident, but he did hold on to the bag of hair.

We were given a full kit of naval issue clothes, including a dress uniform, two sets of whites and two sets of dungarees, and a duffel bag to put it all in.

I found my clothes a little tight but I was told not to worry as we'd be losing weight over the next week. Our "civvies" would be picked up later and sent home in a bag. Within minutes of changing into our new uniform we were told to put our swimming trunks on under a set of dungarees and meet on the tarmac five minutes later.

Five minutes, I was thinking, *are we finally getting a breather?*

But some guy had to yell out, "Why are we putting on the trunks? Are we going swimming? I can't swim, just so you know."

The petty officer who'd been escorting us responded, "Now you have two minutes, so don't be late!" Then he left the barracks.

Everyone was scrambling around and a few even took the time to punch the guy who'd asked the question.

By the time we all found our way out to the tarmac, we were greeted by about half a dozen sailors, shouting at us to line up properly. Then some other guys came out of a barracks next to ours and joined our merry bunch.

Our company commander (the first class petty officer we were assigned to the night before) stepped out in front. "You are all my company and we will be shipmates for the duration of boot camp," he said. "If one of you fails, we all fail. I'm Gunner's Mate First Class Jones, and you should call me 'Gunny' or 'Sir'. From now on, your company will be referred to as 'Sons of a Gunner'."

The other petty officer (a second class), his assistant, unfurled the company flag that we would carry everywhere we went during boot camp. The tallest guy in our group was given the responsibility to not only carry it but to ensure that it never touched the ground. The flag was a deep navy blue with a gold fringe and a picture at the centre of a sailor in dungarees, carrying his rifle by the barrel over his shoulder in a "stepping out" pose. Right above the picture in a curved arc were the words "Sons of a Gunner", and seeing it actually gave me a weird sense of pride.

We were organised into lines according to height, with the tallest at the front and the shortest at the rear. At 5ft 4in, I was at the back of one of the lines. We would be learning how to march. They asked if anyone didn't know their right foot from their left, and amazingly four guys raised a hand. The commander's assistant went to each one and gave them a flat black stone to carry – he put it in their left hand and told them to keep it with them at all times in their hand, pocket or boot, so long as it was in the left to remind them which was which. Now with the command "Left, right, left" we started to attempt to march towards our next destination.

Once we reached the pool, we stripped down to our trunks and were told to jump in the water and keep from the edges, where other guys in trunks were holding long poles. I soon learnt these were used to push away anyone trying to stick close to an edge. Often it meant pushing someone underwater which, as you might imagine, increased their fear.

We treaded water for about 15 minutes though it felt like hours. Eight or ten guys had to be "rescued" by the guys on the outside of the pool. These were the ones who had become so tired that they just sank to the bottom – luckily, none of them were seriously injured.

Then we were on to the next test – a continual swim. Those of us who had survived treading water were instructed to dive in and keep swimming laps until we couldn't carry on or were told to stop by the instructor. At the sound of a pistol shot, off we went. Because treading water had been so taxing many guys only did two or three laps. I reached five before I was pulled out, but five of our guys did nearly 45 minutes of laps!

I later found out that the best swimmers were offered the chance to go to SEAL training, the navy elite, while those who'd found swimming difficult would spend their boot camp days in the pool, rather than marching like the rest of us.

Some of the guys who'd been assigned to "swim companies" told me they could actually swim but their recruiters had told them to pretend they couldn't so they would have an easier time in boot camp. To me, that seemed to show their true characters, and I believed they would carry that same attitude not only through their time in the navy but throughout life in general.

After the swim test those of us who had passed were sent off to meet our "new best friend", or so the escorting petty officer told us. After a short march we arrived at the armoury. Ours was a rifle company which was why the flag showed a character carrying a rifle. As I reached the counter the sailor behind it threw a rifle at me, saying, "Don't drop it."

He then asked me to read off the serial number and sign for the weapon while giving me a well-rehearsed speech about keeping it clean, not losing it and returning it in better condition than I was receiving it. Then it was back outside and in formation for the march back to the barracks, after being shown how to "shoulder" the rifle.

The next eight weeks passed smoothly. We learned to march with precision and looked after our barracks, uniforms and rifles due to regular inspections. We did a variety of physical training exercises and attended a few other classes, such as how to put out different types of fires or going into the gas chamber to see how long we would last once we had taken off our masks.

By far the most interesting part of boot camp was when we went to train on the USS Recruit TDE-1 a fixed scaled-down version of a naval ship that was also commonly known as the USS Neversail. We learnt about tying ropes, climbing ladders on the side of a ship, basic communications and how to go through a hatchway – a doorway to civilians – without knocking ourselves out and taking tests to see if we had any particular skills.

Finally the eight weeks were over and we graduated. Though my company had lost a quarter of the original guys, we did keep all four of those who had arrived in cuffs on that first night. I found out that they had all committed some sort of petty crime (theft, vandalism or smoking marijuana) and the judge had given them the choice of prison or service. Only one really hated it but they were only doing two-year terms, whereas the rest of us had signed up for four to six years.

Before I knew it, the day arrived when we would get orders for our next duty station. I opened my orders and read that I had to report to Balboa Naval Hospital in San Diego to begin training at the US Naval Hospital Corps School. This was just what I'd always wanted.

7

In November 1972, the day after graduation, I reported to Balboa Naval Hospital. Though we'd been offered one week's leave to visit family, I had nowhere to go so decided to stay on the base. Dr Wetmore had sent me one letter during my training only to inform me that he had thrown away everything I owned – my clothes and even the furniture in my room. He signed off the letter with "There is no home for you here."

I was assigned my living quarters so I settled in and took advantage of the days before classes started, becoming familiar with the base and training areas. I also took the opportunity to observe some surgeries. It was clear that if I couldn't cut the medical training I would be made a boatswain's mate and I was sure that wasn't going to happen.

Hospital corpsman training lasted 16 weeks during which time we learned to draw blood and give injections (practising on each other in the class), suturing to close wounds (first on oranges then on pig cadavers as they have a similar resistance to human skin), and learning how to treat multiple wounds (gunshot, burns, stabbings and cuts) and injuries to the eyes, ears, hands and feet.

During our basic surgery training we were even given instructions on delivering babies! All of the instructors were professional and provided quality training. Though the training lasted only 16 weeks, the days often lasted 12 to 16 hours and we had the opportunity to work six days a week if we chose to – which I did.

By about the eighth week the class of 45 went down to 30, of which only five were women. One day, an officer announced that at least a quarter of the men in the class would be assigned to marine corps units and that he would accept volunteers at any time prior to graduation. This was a shock to most of the class but I'd wanted this from the start.

I planned to volunteer as soon as I could. Before the day was over I was approached by six guys at separate times each offering to pay me to volunteer so they wouldn't be chosen. I hadn't mentioned that I was already planning to go with the marines, but being E-1 (the hospital apprentice rating) we were only paid $288 a month and I figured that I could use the extra money.

Sixteen weeks in and just two days before graduating as hospital corpsman, our class now consisted of about 20 to 22 people (all the women had made it). That same officer came to our class to tell us who'd been chosen to go to the marines. First he called out the names of the five who had volunteered and then he informed the class that *all* male graduates would be assigned to marine units, unless they had qualified for an advanced class (know as "C" School).

Of the whole male group, only one of us had been accepted to pharmacy school, and that was the guy who had come to boot camp from jail for smoking marijuana. Right after we had our graduation ceremony we received our orders to go to the field medical service school at Camp Pendleton in Oceanside, California.

I arrived at Camp Pendleton in March 1973, along with all the guys from my corpsman class. We were assigned to Camp Del Mar, Area 21 within the main base, and it was here that we would spend five weeks.

The trainers were "gunnies", seasoned marine gunnery sergeants who in my opinion were by far the meanest and toughest motherfuckers around. The training consisted of another type of boot camp during which we would have to try to prove we were up to the challenge. So not only were we learning advanced field medical skills, we were having to run along sandy beaches (usually for five miles or more), then having to crawl under barbed wire (surrounded by explosions) and run obstacle courses with smoke grenades obscuring our view.

We were also given basic hand-to-hand combat training from a short, slightly overweight Filipino sergeant.

"You're navy piss-ants who don't deserve to be in my presence," he said. "How long before you all cry for your 'mommies'?"

His manner and way of speaking reminded me of Dr Wetmore and I realised that he was yet another bully. So when he asked for a victim to practise on, I stood up. I was just about the smallest guy in the class so probably caught him off guard. But after once more commenting that our class was full of wimps and sissies, he decided to show me what he was going to do.

Quite honestly I got one or two hits on him before spending the better part of 10 minutes being flipped, tossed, punched and lying flat on my back on the mat. What he couldn't believe was that no matter how many times he put me down, I got right up to face him again. He was able to knock me down but something in me wouldn't give him the satisfaction of keeping me down.

Finally with me still on my feet he smiled and told me "good job", before asking for another volunteer. After seeing the beating I'd taken, it was a few moments before someone else stood up. To the credit of the others who faced off with him, they had the sense to stay down after being tossed a couple of times. As it would be shown many times in my life, common sense wasn't my strong suit.

One of the worst parts was that we had to climb a hill known to the basic marines as "Mount Motherfucker" – and even worse, it had to be done while carrying a 50-pound pack. The only good thing was that we weren't doing it in summer when the temperature could be more than 100 degrees fahrenheit. Though the training was hard, it was necessary to produce the type of man needed to fulfil the role of a combat marine. We were told many times during training that a "marine holds his mud", meaning he doesn't ever willingly give up ground. For marines, there's only one direction when on a mission – and that is forwards.

I thought that when this part of training was over I would finally be sent somewhere where my medical training would be useful. But what I was assigned to was a basic "grunt" unit where we went on runs, hikes, dug holes, filled in the holes and were bored all the time. All I was using my medical training for was sunburns, blisters, cigar burns and scorpion stings. As for the last two, it seemed that marines left alone liked to come up with games to prove who was the toughest. Someone thought of placing their forearm against someone else's before laying a lit cigar between them – the winner was whoever could last the longest. Others would carefully tape down scorpions and then arm-wrestle over them – the loser was the person who was stung. Just so you know the US Military didn't approve of these activities and would discipline any marine caught doing something to damage government property – I had to be creative when writing a medical care log so I could protect my fellow men.

Just a little over a month after I'd been assigned to my unit I heard that duty stations were looking for corpsmen. We decided to do the one thing everyone is warned not to do in the military and that is to volunteer. After a couple of interviews, four out of around a dozen of us were selected for recon training. Those who weren't selected felt they'd got the better end of the deal as many of them were posted to foreign embassies.

The four of us who were selected were sent for over a year of jumping out of planes (three to four weeks), scuba school (eight weeks) and jungle warfare school (for about six weeks). The jungle warfare training gave us a taste of what might happen if we were captured and interrogated – the exercises taught us how to survive, escape, resist and evade any situation. Additionally we were trained in small arms, improvised munitions, communications and advanced hand-to-hand combat, including how to use a knife to quickly silence an enemy.

When we weren't being given special training we continued to practise our skills. We would be expected to carry our weight in any marine unit or operations. The two things we would always have to remember were "hold your mud" and the words that had been above our barracks – "Some men fear men, some men fear monsters, and recon is what the monsters fear."

By June 1974, I'd done almost two years of training to turn me into a marine corpsman, and I was ready to go anywhere I was needed. That so happened to be Vietnam with a force recon unit. The combat troops had virtually all been pulled out of the country the previous year so anyone going in now was strictly for classified operations – the principal mission of force reconnaissance was to collect any pertinent intelligence of military importance and to observe, identify and report adversaries to commanders. The force recon units (generally four to six-man teams) operated inland, penetrating deeper into enemy territory from their assigned centre of command. They operated at such great distances that they were beyond the range of any artillery or naval gunfire support. Silence and stealth were vital in reducing the chance of their position being compromised – if a single round was fired, the mission was deemed to have failed. This was why skills in hand-to-hand combat and with a knife had been drilled into us so thoroughly. We were authorised to "terminate a target with extreme prejudice".

I married a woman called Lisa in July 1974, as my marine training was in full swing. I'd told her I would be going overseas but not where, though this marriage was triggered more because I'd been deployed than because we were in love. I didn't tell her I was going to Vietnam, and she wouldn't find out until the following March as I'd sworn an oath to not reveal where I went. Being attached to force recon we were given classified clearance, and as such were able to know things that were of vital importance to American security. To her knowledge I was away on training. The fact that I earned extra pay for being jump and scuba qualified, as well for overseas and hazardous duty, made her quite happy because 90 percent of my pay went to her while I was away.

As a military dependent she was able to shop at the Post Exchange and use all the services that the San Diego bases had to offer, including stores, salons and cinemas. She also had access to the Enlisted Men's Club, which allowed her to drink and socialise with other military wives etc. It would be the "etc" that would later pose a problem in our marriage.

We spent two days in the US Grant Hotel for our honeymoon before she took off her ring and went back to her parents. They hadn't liked me the few times I'd visited and would never approve of our marriage. They would only learn of it when a notice of registration was finally sent to her in February 1975. Her mother opened it as she did all the mail that came to their house. Her parents saw this act of deceit as totally my fault and it would make our marriage even more unsettled, as I was never allowed at their house again.

Back in Vietnam, our main objective was to go deep into the country and try to ascertain enemy movements, to follow up on possible prisoner of war sightings and most importantly, to evacuate members of some of the hill tribes, known as the Degar-Montagnards. During Operation Frequent Wind on 29 March 1975, which was the final phase in the evacuation, I was wounded by a shot to my helmet. I had been processing refugees and helping them on to a C-130 Hercules transport plane (a "Herky Bird"). I was told afterwards that the shot came from somewhere in the brush next to the airfield. Though the bullet didn't penetrate my helmet and enter my skull, it did cause pieces of my helmet to cut my scalp. As I was wearing the chinstrap, the impact of the round caused a whiplash effect on my brain. I was in a coma for about two weeks due to bruising and swelling on my brain. This was my ticket out of Vietnam.

I was in recovery for months, but eventually I was reassigned to work with the ambulance squad out of 32nd Street Naval Station in San Diego. I had hoped this stable duty assignment would strengthen my marriage. I'd learned my wife had committed some infidelities while I was overseas. I made a conscious choice to try to make this marriage work, as I didn't want to fail as a husband.

Most of my duties at this time concerned responding to accidents involving naval or marine personnel, applying emergency medical care and transporting them to Balboa

Naval Hospital. My duties also involved performing sick call at the brig at the naval station. Though I found the work satisfying, I had a longing to return to a marine unit. After a number of requests my wish was finally granted though it wouldn't be to a combat or recon unit as America was deactivating the units and discharging most of the men who had served in them. I wondered what a marine would do in the civilian world when all his training had involved using or firing a machine gun.

My new assignment was actually a big disappointment. Even though I would be serving alongside some former recon marines, we were to become baby-sitters to a diplomat. This wasn't a high-level or even mid-level diplomat – this was somebody's second cousin's brother-in-law who had just about every ailment known to mankind, weighed over 300 pounds and complained about everything. I have no idea what his duties were – he didn't negotiate anything but seemed to just be a delivery boy for documents provided by the US government. The upside to this assignment was that I visited London with him, though I wasn't allowed to travel more than a couple of blocks from the hotel we were staying in. We also took trips to Morocco, Algeria and Libya. For the marines it was a pretty straightforward job – looking out for his security needs and transporting him to his meetings. My part involved getting him ready for the day, so I had to make sure he took his medicine, changed his bandages throughout the day as he had sores from gout and eczema, and try to monitor his blood sugar as he was diabetic.

8

In the autumn of 1976, I learnt that I was to become a father for the first time. I was still signed up to the army but had just been notified that I wouldn't be allowed to renew my naval enlistment for another four years as my skills were combat related and not regarded as suitable for a base hospital or a hospital ship. The day my son David was born was the happiest day in my entire life. It was even more incredible that I could be involved in his delivery, which was a caesarean section. The doctor knew I'd been a corpsman and invited me to assist. Nothing has come close to the joy I felt at the moment I held my son for the first time – I knew I would do anything for him and my family. My past didn't matter, and I could look forward to the future.

By Christmas that year I received an honourable discharge from the US Navy. It was wonderful to be recognised for my service and I felt a sense of tremendous pride. All I ever wanted to do was my duty for my country. But this also meant I was without a job for the first time in my life and with a wife and a baby to support it hit me that I had to find something fast.

While sitting on my own in a Denny's restaurant on Boxing Day I had an idea. I knew it wouldn't sit well with Lisa, but as she was away with her family in Northern California I had a bit of time to get my plans ready. That plan was to open a motorcycle repair shop. I figured I had the mechanical skills from high school and during my time in the navy I'd worked on a number of bikes for other guys. Plus, at the time I was riding a Harley Davidson which I had built from spare parts. So just days later, on 2 January 1977, I walked into a bank in San Diego and asked to speak to a bank manager.

I had no real collateral and the loan manager was reluctant to give me the $3,000 I was asking for. But I couldn't give up on the dream so there and then I took out the photographs of my bike and explained to him that the boxes of parts he was looking at were the bike I was now riding. I couldn't tell if he was impressed or surprised when he saw the photos but he was encouraged by my enthusiasm so eventually granted me the loan, which I was eventually able to pay back in less than 90 days.

I purchased the equipment I needed to set up. Three days later Lisa came home and found that I had turned our garage into a makeshift shop.

"Have you lost your fucking mind?" she asked. "Until you get a real job you can just live in the garage." And with that, she locked me out of the house.

Well, this put a fire under me. I was determined to prove I could make a success of it and in less than a week I had secured a number of bike repair jobs. I thought Lisa would see this was a viable business but the more successful my shop proved to be, the more she refused to have anything to do with it. Lisa would often leave my baby son at the shop with me whenever she wanted to go out. Perhaps she thought it would annoy me and stop me working, but I was actually delighted to have my son there. As the bond between me and my son grew stronger and stronger, the further I drifted from Lisa.

Without telling me, she decided to contact Dr Wetmore. I hadn't seen him since I joined the navy – she wanted to tell him he had a grandson. We'd moved from our apartment above the shop into a new one with a yard in a much nicer neighbourhood. Lisa was sure this would impress Dr Wetmore.

He flew down from Fresno to see our baby but when he saw me he got angry and left. I think Lisa had hoped to get some of the Wetmore money but this seemed a distant possibility as I was sure Dr Wetmore would never part with a single penny. That didn't matter to me – in fact, I was glad to see the back of him – but for my wife this was the final straw.

In June 1977 I came home from work at lunchtime to find my wife waiting for me. She was sat at our kitchen table holding what looked like a paper note. I wondered if it was for me. I could see David was happily sleeping in the next room.

I went to look in on him, and he looked so peaceful there. I knew something was up with Lisa as she could barely bring herself to look at me.

"What's going on Lisa?" I asked, afraid of the answer I knew was coming. After what seemed like hours she began to speak.

"I'm just really tired of being your wife, Jamie. I'm going to go away for some time to think things through. I'll be at my mother's and I promise to be back. I am really sorry, I simply can't do this anymore" she said as she pointed at the space around her.

"OK," I replied. It was hard to get those words out but I knew there was not much I could do to stop her. Once she made up her mind about something, then it was done.

She kissed our boy softly and walked out. Moments later, David started to cry and I did my best to calm him down but I knew then that a tough time was coming for the both of us.

Being in the motorcycle repair business enabled me to meet a variety of people, from fair-weather riders to those who rode with clubs and outlaws. Some of them became my friends. The friendships I formed with other ex-military guys and their families helped me take care of my son and run my shop. I became involved with one group of riders, first as a mechanic, then as a member and finally as their road captain.

I'd been looking after David for four months and was trying my best to be a good father and run a business, when a couple of the guys and their wives suggested we all go out for a night. It was to be a fun evening at a haunted house, raising funds for a local church group. I agreed to go, but only after making sure that David was in good hands.

The haunted house was a typical one, with tombstones, spiderwebs and fog produced by dry ice. As we entered I was up front serving as the leader, with the others following close behind. All was going well until we came to a really thick and heavy plastic curtain. I pushed it aside to reveal strobe lights, the sound of machine gun fire and the smell of gun smoke. Looking to my left, I saw two Viet Cong behind a machine gun. I could see the flashes from the machine gun as each bullet left the barrel. The bodies of US marines were jerking around as the bullets hit them and blood squirted out.

I don't really know what happened, but as I came to I was being dragged into the parking lot, held up by four men including the actor who played one of the wounded marines. They told me I'd lashed out and attacked two actors playing the Viet Cong, beating and kicking them with my hands and feet.

The police sergeant was very understanding when he found out I'd been a marine corpsman and had served in Vietnam during the final days of the war. He was a marine himself.

"Doc, let me take you to the veterans' hospital instead of to the jail," he said.

I agreed and made arrangements with my friends for David to be taken care of before I was taken away. Luckily, no charges were brought against me by the haunted house people. I was admitted for observation for two weeks during which time the doctors kept trying to convince me that the episode hadn't been real, but I was sure it had been – it was one of the most distressing periods of my life.

I was released when they were sure I was no longer a danger to myself or others, but with a diagnosis of extreme post-traumatic stress disorder, PTSD. They recommended that I be given a service disability payment. In fact the US Military Service Review Board ruled that I qualified for 70 percent disability payment for the rest of my life. I couldn't bring myself to accept it though because to do so would mean accepting that I was mentally broken, and I knew if I was seen as crazy they would take my son from me. So I became more isolated, preferring the company of my motorcycles and my son to that of other people.

In the autumn of 1978, out of the blue, a uniformed messenger turned up at my shop while I was working and delivered an invitation to my father's house in Fresno for "Dinner and Discussion". It said that attire would be casual/formal. I was intrigued because we'd had no contact since he'd briefly seen David that time. The wording of the invitation made us laugh in the shop when I read it out.

"Hey, are you going to wear a top hat and tails?" teased Dwarf.

"I think you'll find 'casual/formal' means a suit without a tie," I replied, which brought another round of laughter as no one could imagine me wearing a suit.

I quickly wrote out a note of acceptance and handed it to the messenger, who assured me it would be handed to Dr Wetmore.

On the night of the proposed meeting I turned up at the Wetmore house in my best set of leathers, accompanied by Dwarf and another friend who wanted to see how this meeting was going to go down – I'd told them all about Wetmore and his temper. When he opened the door, he didn't seem surprised that I'd brought people with me.

"This is a family matter," he said. "Your friends are just going to have to wait outside. I do hope you won't mind."

"That may well be but these friends of mine are more family to me than you have ever been, and if they aren't welcome I'm certainly not going to stay," I replied.

"Well in that case," he whispered, so only I could hear what he was saying, "I have some news you might find interesting. Your lovely wife Lisa at the urging of her parents, is planning to file for a divorce and they're going to fight for custody of David. Now with my friends in the judicial system I could prevent her from getting custody, but only if you surrender your parental rights to me. You know that I could give David a bright future with all the advantages you so blatantly squandered. Just think of his future. Think of what you can provide for him and what I could give him in life."

It took me a moment to process what he'd just said before I started to laugh. There was no way I would ever allow him to take care of my son after the way he'd treated me for years. I told him so in no uncertain terms and could see his temper starting to rise as well as his voice.

"Who the hell do you think you are, speaking to me like that!" he yelled.

"I would gladly give my son to Lisa's family before I would ever allow you to go anywhere near David, let alone raise him." I delivered this last line as a final strike against his crazy idea.

"You wait right here. I've got something for you," he shouted at the top of his lungs, turning back into the house and leaving the front door open. He was so angry that Dwarf thought he was going for a gun, but when he came back he threw an envelope into my chest. "I know all about your past," he yelled. "You think you're so special, but you're nothing – you're not my son, and you're not even a US citizen. Now get off my property and never come back." Then he slammed the door in my face. We mounted our bikes and headed back down to San Diego, to shocked to say a word.

We stopped at a service station near Bakersfield to get something to eat. As we sat in a booth I opened the envelope and took out some crumpled documents. Among the paperwork there was what looked like an old British passport for a "Moya Iris Kane" and a worn baptismal certificate for me from a church in the Isle of Man. I had never seen these documents before and didn't know where he'd got them, but the passport had a photo of someone who I thought could be my mother, so I took the picture out and put it in my wallet. I had no idea how to deal with this discovery, so when I got back to San Diego I did the only thing I could and locked the documents away for safe keeping.

I lived in fear of Dr Wetmore's threat but I hadn't heard from Lisa since the day she left us. Then in the spring of 1979, almost two years later, the letter I'd been dreading arrived. I was notified by the superior court in San Jose that she had filed divorce papers and that I would have to appear before the court concerning the custody of my son.

I went to San Jose on the appointed day, taking my son with me as the court had ordered. I also took the Child Protection Services report. In the courtroom I was amazed to find that not only was she represented by an attorney but there was also one representing David, one representing her parents and a fourth representing Dr Wetmore. The only person in the room without an attorney was me. Despite this, I felt confident that things were firmly in my favour.

The judge asked all the parties to present their evidence,

before retiring to his chambers. He deliberated for more than an hour. As he came back into the courtroom, he gave me a look that I took to mean that he was about to give my son back to me but when he started to explain how he came to his decision, what he then said is still seared onto my soul.

"Decisions on the care and custody of a child in these family matters are never easy, but it is the need of the child that supersedes all other concerns," he said. "When I am given a choice between a mother who has a supportive family, and a father who is loving and dedicated to his child but who is a Vietnam veteran who has been diagnosed with PTSD, I have to give the child to the mother."

It felt like somebody had reached deep into my chest and pulled out my heart. My legs started to buckle and I tried to speak but was unable to utter a single word.

"The mother and her family will have full custody of the child," the judge continued. "The father is to be allowed reasonable visitations as long as these are arranged in advance."

I knew this would be the toughest challenge I had ever faced. I lived in San Diego and Lisa and all her family lived between San Jose and Sacramento, in Northern California, so visiting wouldn't be easy. I was also convinced it wouldn't be easy to agree on visitation appointments. And I was right, because after the hearing it would be about nine months before I got to see David again. Every time I called to make arrangements I was given the excuse that he was with one of

Lisa's family members, and my only option was to turn up on her doorstep unannounced if I wanted to see him. One of the most difficult parts of this divorce was that it was finalised on David's fourth birthday.

9

After what happened with Lisa I wasn't prepared to find love but in early 1980 I met a lovely woman called Amy. We'd been seeing each other since just after my divorce, and although losing my son hit me hard I was very pleased to have found her.

Amy and I discovered we were expecting a baby quite soon after getting together which was a pleasant and welcome surprise. I really wanted David to be part of my family again, and as Lisa wasn't accommodating whenever I tried to make arrangements to see him, I had to find another way. With the help of my trusted bike club brother, Dwarf, I decided to drive down and collect David, telling Lisa I wanted him to be at the baby's birth. To my relief, she agreed. David was quite excited to be going on a trip and I told him he would soon be a big brother, which only added to his excitement.

The day my second son, Mark, was born was a beautiful one. David was amazed at how small his brother was, and I was pleased he was able to spend a week and a half with us.

This happiness was short-lived. Soon after David returned to Lisa, she continued to block my visitation rights, and within a few months they moved to an unknown location. I lost David all over again, and there was nothing I could do to get him back – though I tried through the courts and lawyers, it was all in vain.

Amy was from Tulare, about 40 miles south of Fresno. After having Mark, she was feeling very homesick so we decided to move back to Fresno. It was convenient for me as California's Central Valley would be a good location for my shop. Of course my first meeting with Amy's father and stepmother was a disaster. They were Jehovah Witnesses who didn't appreciate that we'd had a child out of wedlock, though they didn't seem to hold it against Mark. As for me, I was a biker and it was obvious from the day I met them that I would never be welcome in their home.

Amy would take Mark to stay with them for the two weeks around Christmas, so he wouldn't be exposed to what they called "pagan" Christmas traditions. This meant that sadly for me, I spent each Christmas on my own. Spending time by myself made me reflect on my life. I went back to the box that contained my documents, still in a crumpled envelope. I decided I was going to take back my birth name of Morgan James Kane, which was on the baptismal certificate. But I wasn't going to spend thousands of dollars hiring an attorney and going through the Californian courts. I didn't have any faith in the system and I already had an idea of how they perceived me when they took my child away. Instead, I chose to adopt the California law that allowed the changing of a name by usage. This meant I would have to change one piece of identification at a time and wait for several months before the next document could be corrected. The simplest one to start with was the GED (General Educational Development), the high school completion certificate equivalent.

I felt positive for the first time in a long time.

10

On 5 April 1981 at about 3am, Amy and I were awoken by a loud knocking. I found our neighbour Tammy, a close friend of Amy's, outside our door. She was crying and hysterical, covered only by a blanket. She frantically blurted out that she'd just been raped and the man who had done it was still in the house with her children. She begged us to call the police.

"Tammy, listen to me," I said. "Where are your children?"

"I think they're still asleep upstairs in their bedroom, but the man who did this is armed," she answered through her sobs. "He has a knife."

I turned to Amy. "Amy, call the police now. I'll go and make sure that the kids are safe."

"Jamie, wait – do you want the shotgun?" she asked.

"No – he's only got a knife?" I replied, and walked towards next door.

I believed my military training in hand-to-hand combat and knife fighting would be enough to confront the man.

Who knew how a situation with a shotgun would evolve, and I knew I could disarm him without having to hurt him.

When I arrived at the house I saw him standing on the front porch, looking around. I shouted at him to come down and face me, but instead he stepped back into the house. When he did come out again, he tried to walk away from me. I moved forwards. As I did, he pulled a ten-inch butcher's knife from behind his back and slashed towards my stomach. I blocked him and successfully disarmed him after around 30 seconds of struggle. I threw his knife a few feet away and held him down until the police arrived. When he was arrested and taken away, we were all relieved, especially when we found the children safe in their beds.

After this incident, life went back to normal, although Amy's parents were beginning to put pressure on me to marry Amy and make our son legitimate. I resisted at first as I worried it would be a repeat of my earlier failed marriage, but when they informed me they'd made all the arrangements and all I had to do was to show up, I agreed. After all, I loved her. However, there was only one slight problem: my driver's licence was still in the name Wetmore, which was considered to be my legal name and consequently, it was the one that Amy took for her last name. Finally, right after my son's second birthday in 1982, I had my driver's licence changed to my true name, Morgan James Kane – another reason to celebrate.

By this time I had a well-established motorcycle repair shop called Sunrise Cycles. I specialised in the restoration of pre-1960 motorcycles of all makes and models. I had contacts across the US who would let me know if they found useful parts, and I'd developed a wide circle of biker friends and acquaintances. So it wasn't unusual when, in May 1982, a friend called to tell me an owner in West Covina wanted to sell some parts.

I arranged to drive with Dwarf down to look at the parts in question, meeting at our favourite Denny's restaurant. As we sat waiting for the guy to arrive, four girls entered the restaurant and sat in the booth next to ours. One of the girls kept looking at my repair shop vest. Then the guy we were waiting for pulled up outside in his truck. As Dwarf and I got up to leave I overheard the girl say to her friends, "I had a brother whose nickname was Sunrise, but then my mother left me and they both disappeared."

Outside, I could tell immediately that this guy had very little knowledge of the parts he was selling. So I couldn't pass up this deal and paid him the asking price – about half what the parts were worth. While Dwarf was putting the parts in our truck, I went back inside to order us more coffee.

One of the girls from the table started talking to me. "Do you know a Tricia Kearns?" one asked.

It had been more than a decade since I'd heard the name, so it took me a moment to reply.

"Yes, my mother was married to a man named Kearns."

The other three girls came over and surrounded me. The girl who'd mentioned she'd had a brother called Sunrise said she was Tricia Kearns, whose father Daniel had been married to a woman called Moya. I was in a state of shock and had to sit down, but I wanted to know more.

We spoke for over an hour. Tricia told me she was living with her Uncle John and her son, Joey. She had lost contact with her two sisters, Janet and Pamala. As we talked, it became clear that she was my baby sister Tricia, whom I hadn't seen since she was just a few months old. She invited me and Dwarf to come over to her house to meet John and Joey, and we accepted.

Their house looked like a trash heap. Dirty clothes were strewn all over the living room, dishes were piled up in the sink and there was a strong smell of dirty nappies. On meeting Uncle John, I realised he was Stanley John Kearns, Tricia's father's brother, who I'd met when I was a child. Apparently he'd adopted her after her father had died, so even though she was his adopted daughter, she still called him "Uncle John".

Our conversation turned to me – I told them that I lived a quiet life in Fresno with a wife and two-year-old son. As Tricia wanted to move out of their neighbourhood, she suggested that it might be nice to move to Fresno and be near family. Since the loss of my mother and David, I found the idea of reconnecting with family quite appealing so without a second thought, I welcomed it. Not even a month had gone by when she called me to say they had rented a place in Fresno but needed help to drive the truck containing all their furniture and property. John didn't have the right licence, apparently.

A couple of days later, I caught the Greyhound bus to West Covina and met with them. The truck was already loaded, so all I had to do was hitch their car to the back of it. With Tricia, John and Joey in the cab with me, we made the 250-mile drive back to the apartment they had rented in Fresno.

When we arrived and I opened the back of the truck to start unloading. I found an infestation of hundreds, if not thousands of cockroaches in the boxes as Tricia had packed up all the dirty dishes and clothes together. I closed the truck and went to get some bug bombs to kill the infestation. Lucky for Tricia most of her furniture was plastic coated, though she wasn't happy with the prospect of having to wipe down everything to remove the poison. John insisted that since I'd had all their property quarantined in the truck, I should pay for a motel room that night. I was willing to help. Tricia was my family.

Tricia and John argued a lot and, trying to help, I let him spend time in my shop. However this didn't turn out to be such a good idea, as he spent most of his time with a can of beer in his hand, trying to tell me how to run my business. He was even worse when I wasn't there – he acted as if he had part-ownership and tried to order around my employees and demanded they buy beer for him. In February 1983, he'd been harassing my counter girl so much that I had to ban him from Sunrise Cycles. While he'd been coming to my shop I seemed to have a lot of problems with my bikes, but they all cleared up once he was no longer around.

After this, John started carrying a cane, but it wasn't because he had problems walking – it was because he hid a two-and-a-half-foot-long sword inside it, I found out. He would often carry a hunting knife and a pistol too. His drinking got worse, and on several occasions he came to my house in a terrifying state. One time, he pulled the knife on me so I had to disarm him by putting him in a sleeper hold as I'd been trained to do. At no time did I mean to cause him any permanent harm, but it was clear that his ego was bruised and he'd often tell me that "one day I'd get mine". Neighbours called the police on some of these occasions and various reports were filed. But as I wasn't willing to press charges, no one was arrested.

On 4 June 1983, I was out of town at a motorcycle swap meet in Yuma, Arizona. When I called home to check in with Amy, she told me that John had been arrested for hitting Tricia. The police had discovered his concealed weapons, including the sword in the cane, a small pistol and a knife in his belt buckle. Tricia and Amy told the District Attorney that John had also choked two-and-a-half-year-old Joey in the previous month, and it had taken both of them to pull him off. Luckily Joey hadn't suffered any serious injury, but it added yet another charge against him. Amy had kept this information from me fearing it would cause an even worse altercation with John. Tricia also told the District Attorney that over the past few months John had taken about 400 dollars of her welfare money by force.

About a week later while John was in the county jail, Tricia told the District Attorney that John had called her and said he would kill her when he got out. She was terrified, he had already threatened her a number of times. In the first week of July, despite all the charges and that he met none of the criteria to secure his release, John was released with a restraining order that decreed he wasn't to go near either Tricia or Joey.

On 12 July 1983, a little after 11pm, I arrived home after spending the day helping a friend build a house. As I pulled my truck into the driveway I noticed all the lights were off including the porch light. This was unusual. I also noticed Amy's car wasn't in the drive. I knew she couldn't have called me even if something had happened, because we weren't near any phones at the construction site. I unlocked the front door and went inside. I turned on the living room light. Right there in the middle of the floor was Stanley John Kearns lying motionless. I called my wife's name and ran to our bedroom. It was all in order. Going back to the living room, I bent over him to see if he was still breathing – he wasn't. He was stone cold.

I slowly rolled him over, looking for a wound, but I couldn't find one. He was definitely dead and had been for a while. But why was he at my house? And where were my wife and son? I'd told Amy not to let him come round, so why had she ~~did she know~~ he was here? I should have called the police but they knew he and I had a volatile history. What would I say to them? Would they believe me when I said I'd just come home and found him there dead? I knew if I did that, I'd end up going to jail.

All I could think about was getting John's body away from the house and my family. So I found a sleeping bag to put him in. While carrying him out to my truck, a car's headlights shone across the drive.

"I took Mark to a friend's house for the night," Amy said as soon as she saw me. "John turned up drunk saying he was hungry so I cooked him dinner. Then after, I gave him his bottle of asthma capsules and he took one. He stood up then collapsed like he was having a fit."

Tricia had given these capsules to Amy when John was arrested, asking Amy to take them to John in jail. But the jail wouldn't allow prisoners to have any medicines that hadn't been prescribed by a doctor so Amy had brought them home with her.

"Why didn't you call the police?" I asked.

"I panicked and thought he'd got sick from the dinner I cooked," she replied. "Besides, it looked like he was having an epileptic fit and they always get better. I was afraid he'd be mad at me, so thought it would be best to leave him. Figured he'd be gone when I got home… So what are you going to do? How are you going to fix this?"

Funnily enough, looking back, she didn't ever ask me if he was dead. I told her we had to get him away from the house. She helped me load him on to the truck's bed and we closed the tailgate. She jumped into the cab with me and I pulled out into the night not knowing where I was headed.

"Did you bring a shovel?' Amy asked a few minutes later. I hadn't.

"So what are you going to do with his body?"

She asked so many questions and I had no answers so my responses made her angry. I'd lost track of the time and even where we were. I remained focused on driving. All I could think was that it would soon be daylight and I had a dead body wrapped in a sleeping bag in my truck bed.

By 4:30am, Amy had stopped screaming at me. I saw a place by a field where I could pull over. Once we'd stopped, we took out the body and placed it near a post where John would easily be found. I rolled him over and slipped a piece of paper into his wallet that said, "in case of emergency" and wrote down my name and shop's phone number. Then we sat him up, got back into the truck and drove away.

John was found at about 6:30am.

Amy and I didn't speak about the incident – I dropped her off at home and went to the shop, where I busied myself with the bikes. I didn't even think to tell Tricia. At about 1pm that afternoon Tricia called me to say police detectives had been to see her and it finally hit me that the previous night had actually happened. Somehow my mind had made me believe it was a terrible nightmare though I couldn't remember when I'd last slept.

At nearly 3pm, detectives showed up at my shop – the piece of paper had led them to me. "Why did I put that paper in his wallet?" is a question I've asked myself my whole life. Was it out of remorse that he was dead and we hadn't been on better terms? Was it, as I've told others, that I wanted to be sure he was identified so he would receive a proper burial? To this day, I really don't know.

I told the detectives I hadn't seen him since before his arrest and that I didn't even know he had been released from jail. But Amy told Tricia that I'd picked John up the day before and driven him to my house where she served him dinner. Then I'd driven him to the Greyhound bus station as he'd planned an out-of-town trip. Tricia had told all this to the detectives. This information caught me so off guard that I had no idea how to respond. But I just said I didn't know what they were talking about and that I had to get back to work.

After they left I tried to figure out what was going on, so I called Amy.

"They're here now," she said. "What should I do?"

"Just act dumb and admit to nothing," I replied. "We'll sort this," was the only response I had on offer.

Not wanting to rouse any suspicion from the detectives I chose to wait a couple of hours before going home. Once I got there Amy and I talked about what the detectives had said.

"I called Tricia shortly after you dropped me home and told her everything that happened," she said, to my amazement. "Couple of hours later Tricia called me back. Told me what to tell the police – that I picked Uncle John up and brought him home, gave him dinner and then took him to the bus station."

Tricia told Amy that an autopsy would find what John had eaten the night before. The police would know it was a home-cooked meal, which would implicate Amy, as he wasn't allowed around Tricia's house. Now I was completely confused, I had to call Tricia.

"I didn't tell Amy to say anything like that," she said. "In fact, Amy told me what to say if the police came by."

Who was lying, and why?

A day later, Tricia called me in hysterics.

"I need to know how John died," she said. "I loved him and miss him terribly." I heard wailing in the background. "And Joey's crying too because I've just told him about Uncle John. You're my older brother, so can't you contact the police to find out if they've done an autopsy yet? And find out when I can sort out his burial."

Against my better judgement I did as I was asked and made the call to the police. I was referred to the coroner's office. They told me they would send a full report to the detectives assigned to the case, who would be in touch – if not, I should contact them in a few days. I asked when John's body would be released. Again I was told vaguely that a decision would be made sometime after the autopsy report had been given to the detectives.

On 4 August 1983, both Tricia and Amy were arrested for forgery. The police said on 7 July 1983, five days before John would be found dead, Tricia had forged two cheques from Stanley John Kearns' bank account totalling $440 and Amy had driven her to the bank. A handwriting expert concluded that Tricia had filled out the cheques and endorsed them, trying to conceal she had forged his name. Tricia had told the police John took money from her, which to the detectives was a motive for the crime. Since Amy had driven Tricia and been given money for petrol, this made her an accessory to the forgeries, as she'd received ill-gained funds.

Later that day I was arrested too, charged with murder. According to the autopsy, the cause of death was "suffocation", and the police believed I had strangled John. Amy's parents were able to take custody of Mark, though Joey had to go into a county care facility.

Now the circus began.

Amy changed her story accusing Tricia of killing her adoptive father and forcing her to do the forgeries. Tricia said Amy had given me some of the money from the forgery which suddenly saw me charged as an accessory too. We were soon given attorneys. But because my wife and I were co-defendants the public defender's office could only represent one of us and I drew the short straw. Both Tricia and Amy were appointed private practice attorneys. My wife was represented by Ernest Kinney, known to be one of the finest attorneys in Fresno with an excellent win record. I was given a public defender. The public defenders did such a bad job in defending cases that they were commonly known by the nickname "prison dispatchers". Mine turned out to be an inexperienced woman who, so far, had only handled minor juvenile cases, even though I was facing a capital case of murder.

On 5 August, we each had bail placed on us at $500,000. Unable to pay it we sat in jail waiting for what might come next. Amy had given permission for the detectives to search our vehicles and house before discussing it with her attorney. During the search of our house, the detectives seized a number of important papers, including my baptism certificate and my mother's British passport.

At first, I was put in one of the jail's general population tanks. But when the actual murder charge was filed, I was moved into the "high power" section of the jail, which was reserved for prisoners considered to be the most dangerous and violent. These were four-man cells, though they usually had six men in them, which meant two people had to sleep on the floor under the bottom bunks. High power, like the rest of the jail, wasn't segregated by race. The cell I was placed in already contained three black guys and two Hispanics, so I thought I would be one of the ones sleeping on the floor. But I was wrong.

"Sunrise?" said one of the young black guys. "I can't believe it's you, bro – what they get you for?" He pulled one of the Hispanics and his mattress off his bottom bunk and threw them on the floor, telling him he would be sleeping under the bunk, as this was now mine. "We need another mattress in here," he hollered to the cop.

He immediately pulled me in and gave me a hug. "This is Sunrise, a cool biker who owns a shop where my uncle, Big Bird, goes," he said to the other two black guys.

I realised who he was – Skeeter. We had met on a number of occasions when I visited the clubhouse of the motorcycle club that his uncle belonged to. On a few occasions I'd helped Skeeter fix his car and dirt bike for free.

This friendship would make my next four months, before Skeeter was sent to prison, a little easier. It was unfortunate that this eighteen-year-old was going to serve life without parole for killing a drug dealer who had been selling drugs at his little sister's school.

Finally, on 1 September, we were granted a reduction in our bail terms. Amy's was lowered to $5,000 as she was only charged with being an accessory to forgery, and her parents quickly paid it. Tricia's was down to $10,000 for forgery and her attorney was able to pay 10 percent to a bail bondsman, which secured her release. My bail was reduced to $250,000 but the District Attorney's office had asked the court to freeze all my assets.

Over the next month and a half, it was one court postponement after another, while the District Attorney tried to decide how to get convictions on the most charges for each of us. My attorney assured me that their case was circumstantial at best. She believed my charges would either be dropped or reduced down to involuntary manslaughter, which "only" carried a two to four year term. On 7 October, the District Attorney informed Tricia that he was looking at getting her an 18-year sentence for the forgeries – he said it was especially callous because she had done it to her own adoptive father. Then, on 10 October, Tricia's attorney contacted the District Attorney, saying that her client had new and vital information to the case and she would like to work a deal. The District Attorney arranged for the detectives to meet Tricia at her attorney's office.

Tricia stated that Stanley John Kearns hadn't been strangled as the autopsy showed, but had in fact been poisoned by cyanide. She said that Amy had put the poison in the asthma capsules. When the jail wouldn't take the medicines,

Amy had chosen to keep the capsules and invited John over to the house for dinner. Amy had hoped John would take a capsule and then get up and leave. But instead he died on my living room floor. Amy had told Tricia that all I did was move the body. Tricia was the sole beneficiary of Stanley John Kearns' life insurance policy, which was estimated at about $50,000. She believed that Amy killed him because of his abuse towards Tricia and Joey. She also said Amy expected a share of the inheritance. Tricia had, in fact, received his life insurance benefits while waiting for trial, and spent most of it within 10 days of receiving it.

On 13 October, a second autopsy was conducted by the same pathologist, and he reported that cyanide had indeed been the cause of death. Tricia was given full immunity on the forgery charges, providing she gave "truthful" testimony. Later that day Amy was re-arrested and placed back in jail, now charged with first-degree murder. My charges of murder were dropped and replaced with an accessory to murder charge for moving his body from the house – they thought I was covering up my wife's crime.

On 19 October, Tricia admitted to lying to the police before her statement on the tenth. It also transpired that she'd confided in a friend, Jerry Root, back in July. He admitted to the court that Tricia's attorney had advised him not to say anything until the case went to trial. During this hearing, Amy's attorney pointed out that Tricia had the most to gain from Stanley John

Kearns's death – Tricia had accused him of abusing her and her son and of taking her money, she was the one who had him arrested, she gave Amy the medicines to take to him in jail, she forged his cheques and was the sole beneficiary of his life insurance policy. Yet the judge didn't feel this was a compelling argument, and nor did the District Attorney feel she'd violated her agreement for immunity. The murder case against my wife went ahead – and I could do nothing more than watch.

The new charges placed on Amy caused her a lot of stress. So our attorneys arranged for us to have an hour-long visit behind glass every Sunday, where I would try to boost her spirits. Her parents would also bring Mark up to see her every Saturday, and she would let me know how he was doing. Then, on 30 November, the bottom really fell out of our world.

The District Attorney upped Amy's charges to first-degree murder with two counts of "special circumstances" (the poison and the monetary gain), which meant she could face the death penalty if convicted. He also put the two counts of forgery on to Amy (even though he had proof that Tricia had done this on her own), as well as two counts of attempted forgery (being the person who drove Tricia when she cashed the cheques).

It wasn't until 4 December that Amy showed me her new charge sheet, pressing it up against the glass that separated us. I saw a fragile, frightened girl and not the angry and self-absorbed woman I'd lived with for the past few years. She kept asking me to help her, saying she didn't want to die.

"Mark will grow up with everyone knowing I'd been sent to death row," she said. "This will scar him for life. You can fix this. Don't you love me? Don't you love our son? What will he think of you if you let me die?"

Our time was up and we returned to our cells. After that day she refused to see me again, sending word through the guards that it was too painful, knowing I "was going to let her down when she needed me most". All I could think about were those questions she had asked on that last visit.

On 21 December, Amy went to trial and Tricia testified against her. The trial lasted only a couple of days, breaking for Christmas. Just before New Year, the verdict was back. It was a hung jury, because one person had a problem with a woman and a mother being sentenced to death. Though this was a small victory for Amy and her attorney, the District Attorney immediately re-filed the charges and began the process of picking a new jury that he expected to return a solid conviction.

In the second week of January 1984, I was called out for a visit with my attorney and my wife's attorney. They told me I was being offered a "one time and only one time" offer to save my wife's life. The District Attorney had agreed that if I pleaded guilty to the first-degree murder charge, the two forgery charges and the two attempted forgery charges, he would drop all charges against my wife so she could be with our son. Even though the sentence would be 25 years to life, I would be eligible to be released in 12 and a half years with good behaviour and he wouldn't oppose parole.

"If you save Amy's life, her love for you will be stronger," said my wife's attorney. "You will have more respect from your son than most fathers could hope for. This deal would mean you'll be out of prison to see your son graduate from high school. And besides, you've faced worse and survived in Vietnam. How do you think your wife would survive on death row?"

He said it was my choice and hoped I was man enough to make the right decision. Then he left me alone with my attorney. She confirmed that the District Attorney had indeed made the offer. I had about 30 minutes to make my decision.

I can honestly say I thought for a brief moment that I was about to be really screwed. But I had to make a decision and that decision would alter my life forever. I told my attorney that I would agree to the terms if she believed the District Attorney would keep his word. She assured me he would. She then produced a paper for me to sign, agreeing to change my plea.

The following week I faced a judge and felt like I had been punched in the stomach. I took responsibility for the murder, the forgeries and the attempted forgeries. After the hearing, sentencing was set for mid-February, and my attorney said she planned to try and get me a shorter sentence. I later wondered how the whole judicial system couldn't see the whole process was a sham. There was no evidence – I hadn't had any involvement in the forging of the cheques and didn't even know about them. I certainly couldn't have been involved in either of the attempted forgery charges, as I hadn't even been in the state at the time. As far as the murder, I had moved the body and lied to the police, but it had been proven in Amy's first trial that Stanley had purchased the cyanide. Tricia and Amy had handled the capsules, yet neither of them had admitted to being in possession of the poison.

By mid-February 1984, I was still waiting to be sentenced. Amy didn't want to see me until she knew I was going through with it and that she be released. The District Attorney hadn't yet dropped Amy's charges as I hadn't yet been sentenced and could still technically change my mind if I wanted to. My attorney did ask the judge to give me a shorter sentence, but her pleas fell on deaf ears. When she told him I had served in the military and had been given an honourable discharge, he responded, "That was certainly a mistake, as there is nothing honourable about you." But she did get him to grant me the right to be placed under my birth name of Morgan James Kane, with John Wetmore to be listed as "AKA".

The Friday before I was sent to prison, the District Attorney tried to pull a fast one by offering my wife the same deal I'd taken, just as they were giving their closing arguments and sending the jury off to deliberate. Amy refused, as advised by her attorney who, in turn, produced my change of plea in his closing statement. He told the court I'd taken responsibility for all the charges, even that I had lied under oath about my wife knowing nothing about the murder. It took less than an hour for the jury to come back with "not guilty" on Amy's murder and forgery charges, though they did find her guilty for the attempted forgeries. I saw my wife two days later and she thanked me for freeing her from most of the charges.

"You've done the right thing, Jamie. You have nothing to worry about," my attorney assured me as we watched my wife leave the room. "Things always work out in the end."

Of course it wasn't my attorney who was going to prison, and I don't think she had any idea what I would face.

PART 2

California Medical Facility – Vacaville

It was 27 February 1984, the day I was going to prison. This didn't yet seem real to me   it was just words on a piece of paper. At 2:30am, the sheriff's deputy started banging on the bars to wake everyone up, even those who weren't being transferred to prison or court.

For me it was just a formality as I hadn't slept and had only had catnaps since the day I was sentenced. Not because I was scared, but more because I knew what was going to happen. I was preparing my mind, much as I did when I was in the military going on ops, or when riding into some other motorcycle club's territory. You have to awaken your heightened awareness. It was this ability to take in my surroundings quickly and assess the risk of danger that would become vitally important to my survival in prison.

At 3:00am, those of us who were to get in the vans were told to "be dressed and have all your personal property in your hands, as you can't come back." We were all escorted to the chow hall for breakfast; for those without a bus ride or court appearance, this wouldn't be until 6:00am. When we reached the chow hall doors, a county correctional officer separated those going to prison (already sentenced and designated as "convicted") from those going to court (so far only detained). We, the convicted, were seen as the "dangerous ones".

The food that morning was chicken gravy on toast, hot rice cereal (cooked to the consistency of glue), a battered apple, a frozen orange juice cup, half a pint of milk and burnt coffee. If you didn't know better, you might think this was an additional punishment because we were convicted, but it was a common meal in the Fresno County Jail.

At about 6:30am, the county correctional officer came back to get us. We walked down the stairs to the holding tank opposite the intake and release counter, which was where they kept everyone's personal belongings while they were processed into custody. Now we were reversing that procedure.

At exactly 8am, the grated window was opened, revealing a county correctional officer with the grumpiest-looking face I'd ever seen. He had a poor excuse for a crew cut and was unshaven with a bulbous red nose and a stubby cigar butt hanging from his lips. He called us up to the window, one by one in alphabetical order, to receive our clothes. These were the same clothes we'd been arrested in and they hadn't been washed just stuck in a paper bag and placed on a shelf in some warehouse.

When my name was called, I went to get my bag. On opening it the musty smell of dirt and sweat wafted out and I found my dirty, grease-stained jeans, black t-shirt and cowboy boots still inside. If it had just been mine it would be bad enough, but this was combined with the smell of 10 other guys whose clothes had been in varying states of cleanliness when they were arrested.

The only person who didn't get a bag was a young guy with long blond hair who looked like a California surfer but without the tan. When they called him up, he was out of alphabetical order, so it seemed like the officer wanted everyone to focus on him. The county correctional officer passed the kid a box and remarked, "Someone must be special." It turned out the box contained new clothes: silk underwear and undershirt, an Italian suit and shoes that looked like they were made of snakeskin.

As the kid started to get dressed one of the other guys in our group decided to ask him about his fancy duds – they had tags still on them and were certainly not what you would expect anyone to wear to prison. The young guy replied that his parents had brought them, as he'd been arrested at the club and was wearing Speedos and slippers at the time. His comment brought murmurs from within the group – everyone seemed to disapprove, on one level or another. Then the kid started to explain that he had sensitive skin and could only wear silk underclothes, so had suffered terrible rashes from the jail clothes he'd been forced to wear for the last year. That comment brought on some condescending laughs.

We were ushered into another room to wait. I noticed a number of guys had taken an interest in the kid. They were asking him about his family and he was all too willing to tell them until it came to his charges, which he said were "frivolous and had been blown out of perspective". He told them that under the advice of his attorney he wasn't to discuss the elements of his case, which he'd been assured would be overturned very quickly – he expected to be in Europe by the summer.

At the cashier's window we received any money and valuables that had been held for us in the safe. Most of us had a few hundred dollars if we were lucky, but when it came to the kid we were all amazed when he was given $10,000. As you can imagine, every eye in the room was on him and his wallet – even those of the guards. Then we walked into the sally port area where waist chains and handcuffs were put on us, and the 12 of us were loaded onto a van with two guards to escort us to prison. A sergeant followed in a car to ensure that no one tried to escape.

The drive from Fresno to Vacaville took about two hours. Most guys in the van had been to prison before – they were laughing and joking about seeing their friends when they got there. Only the kid, an older guy and I stayed quiet during the trip. When we reached Vacaville, we were taken to the

California Medical Facility: this wasn't only a fully functioning medical hospital but also where inmates were trained to work as nurses' aides, x-ray technicians and lab technicians in the "free world".

As the van approached the gate we saw a young couple kissing on a bench. At first it appeared to be a guy and a girl, but then I realised this was an all-male prison and saw they were both wearing prison blues. The kid was quite shocked to see this, which amused most of the other guys, and they teased him that with his long hair he could easily go "girlie".

We were taken off the van one by one, unshackled and taken inside to be processed. We were told to strip naked and place our clothes in the boxes in front of us. We were then told to place our valuables and money in an envelope with our name written on the front. Within minutes we had all complied, except for the kid who had chosen not to remove his underpants or vest. When one of the prison guards noticed, he walked over to him and slapped him on the back of the head, knocking him to the floor. The guard told the kid to get up and get naked or he would knock him down again. At this point, the kid promptly did as he was told.

One of the biggest differences between the county jail and this state prison was the way in which we were searched. In jail, they would make us get naked to check we weren't concealing anything on our bodies, get us to shake our hair and look in our mouths and that was it. Prison was different.

Now we were standing around naked, a guard made us run our fingers through our hair vigorously, open our mouth and stick out our tongue, before they lifted it and moved it from side to side. Then they had us lift our genitals and turn around and lift each foot. Finally we had to bend over, pull our butt cheeks apart and cough three times to check we hadn't put anything up inside.

Once the guard was finished, we were called up one by one, still naked, to bring over our valuables to an inmate helping the guards. This inmate counted our money and called out the amount to a prison guard. We then signed for it, and the envelope was sealed and sent to the prison office. When they reached the kid and the inmate shouted out $10,000, the whole room went silent. A sergeant came out of the office and went over to the inmate to verify what he'd heard, before asking the kid to follow him, still naked, back into his office. Once the rest of us had signed for our money, we were issued with the fluorescent green uniform of reception inmates.

We were told to sit on some benches and wait for a guard at the intake desk. When the kid rejoined our group, it looked like he'd been crying, and he wouldn't hold eye contact with any of us. I found out later that the sergeant had threatened him. If the kid tried to tell his family or any other staff about being struck by the guard, the sergeant would put him in with someone who would rape him daily. That was his welcome to the California Department of Corrections.

The intake guard called out "Wetmore".

I told him my name was Kane.

"It says Wetmore on your abstract of judgement, the ticket from court authorising your transport to prison," he said.

I looked down at the document, which said, "True name: Morgan James Kane" followed by "AKA or name on indictment: John Raymond Wetmore". I pointed this out to him.

He gave me a stern look and tapped his badge. "I'm in charge around here," he said. "I wear the badge and I have the keys, and I say your name is Wetmore."

I tried to reason with him, explaining that Kane was my birth name and Wetmore had been an adopted name but I changed my name back to Kane by usage. All that achieved was a puzzled look, and he told me I could appeal if I didn't like it.

"So Wetmore," he asked. "Have you been a guest of the State of California before?"

"No, I haven't."

"Well where did you serve time then? All those tattoos, you must have been a prisoner somewhere."

"I haven't done any prison time anywhere," I insisted.

He gave me a look that showed he didn't believe me. "You can lie all you want, but when we run your prints we will know your full record," he responded.

There was no way I was going to get this guard to change his mind, so figured I would wait until I could speak to someone with more brains and less ego.

Finally after about 30 minutes, the guard said we were done. He gave me an index card with my prison inmate identification number and my unit and cell numbers. Then told me to remember the ID number as it would be mine for the rest of my life. Going back to the benches to wait for the others to be processed, I remember looking at the card and seeing "C-81562". The lyrics from a Johnny Rivers song ran through my mind – it's true when they give you a number they take away your name.

At about 8pm, the 12 of us from Fresno and another 15 or so guys from various county jails in northern California were all finally processed. We hadn't been fed since breakfast. At some point we were given a cardboard box containing a meal and a bedroll (containing one sheet, one blanket and one towel) and escorted to our reception housing units. As we walked down the long corridor I tried to remember each door, making a mental map. Finally we got to 'T' Unit, and 10 names were called out. These 10 were told to step up to the door where two guards were waiting for them. The rest of us carried on walking.

We arrived at U Unit and another 10 names were called, including "Wetmore". Just hearing that grated on me but I figured I'd get it fixed the next day. Just as before, two guards showed us to our cells, while the final remaining inmates walked on. One guard took the three of us up to the third floor and our cell doors. "When the lights are turned on in the morning, you have three minutes to get up and get dressed before chow. Open up cell 347!" he shouted to another guard. I walked in and the door closed behind me with a resounding thud.

Days seemed to follow a rigid routine and day three started much the same: lights on at 5am, doors opening, everyone rushing to chow, me sitting with the others and my cellmate sitting with the Whites, who I could see were asking him about me. Then I went back to the cells and waited to see what would happen next.

My cellmate and I spoke only a few words before going back to bed, something that's common in prison when you have nothing else going on. I started reading a western by Louis L'Amour that one of the guys at my dining table had passed to me. I'd been reading for about an hour when the cell door opened again.

"Wetmore, come out here." A man in a suit and another in a captain's uniform stood in the doorway.

I stood up, put my shoes on and left the cell. They walked me down to the chow hall and sat with me at one of the tables. Then the captain pulled out a file.

"I'm the chief medical officer and this here is the captain of this institution," said the man in the suit. "Is it true you were a navy corpsman?" After I confirmed it was, he asked me to tell him about my training and the injuries I'd treated. "I want him," he said to the captain after a while.

"Would you like to work in the hospital as a ward aide?" the captain asked me. "We may also need you to act as surgical technician. You'll still be an orientation inmate but will wear blues and have the same privileges as all mainline inmates, as long as you go to all your orientation appointments and don't abuse any privileges."

I immediately agreed – I knew if I stayed in the reception unit, I would spend a lot of time locked in a cell. To be able to move around the prison and get an understanding of what lay ahead of me seemed a simple choice. I was taken back to my cell but within a couple of hours the door opened and after giving my cellmate the book I was reading, I started my journey to the "blue side".

As I crossed over from reception, everyone was looking at me. It became apparent that a green becoming a blue wasn't a common sight. The first stop was the clothing room where I was given brand new clothes, new boots and a full bed roll, including two sheets, two blankets, a pillow and case, two towels and a hygiene bag. Then I was taken down to my new housing, which turned out to be a dormitory. It was a 26-man dorm yet it only at present contained 12 men. These were all workers in the hospital or in a trade such as plumbing, electrical or maintenance so they weren't there when I arrived. The guard told me to take any empty bunk and report to the hospital entrance.

Dressed in my overalls, I was met by a rather tall, effeminate guy with large breasts. He was wearing extremely tight jeans and a shirt that had obviously been altered to fit his figure.

"My name is Sizzle," he said in high-pitched voice. "I run the ward for the post-op and paralysed patients. You'll be working for me."

Sizzle showed me around, explaining the needs of each patient on the ward, where the medical supplies were kept and how to complete the different logs. After a quick pat on the shoulder, he said, "Welcome to the team" and left.

That first weekend on the blue side, I decided to go to the movies, which were shown on a screen in the gym. The seating was on bleachers used for basketball games or music shows. I bought a soda, a bag of popcorn and a Snickers bar, and went into the gym with a few hundred others. The movie was *48 Hours* with Eddie Murphy and Nick Nolte. I noticed a glint of light to my left, turned and saw a guy with a knife hidden under his jacket. Not knowing his intentions, and as people were still coming in, I moved to where my back was against the wall and I could see anyone approach.

The lights went down and the movie started, but I couldn't stop thinking about the guy I'd seen with the knife. As we were all leaving, I noticed someone in the front row slumped over with a jacket over his shoulders. Moments after getting out into the hallway, I heard the guards' whistles and the order to "get on the wall", as they ran past us to the gym.

It turned out that the victim had taken the "girlfriend" of the person with the knife to the movie and paid with his life. This was the first killing in prison while I was there but it wouldn't be the last.

My first job involved changing dressings on the patients with bed sores. During the day, I learnt that almost every-one working on the ward was referred to as a "queen", a homosexual man who wore make up and tried to be as feminine as possible. I was also told that the queens had all the powerful roles throughout the institution, so even the most homophobic guy would hold his tongue. I'd lived in San Diego for many years and had met a lot of gay people. But I'd never seen so many queens in one place at the same time. It was very obvious that the staff were giving them the best jobs.

About a week after I started working in the hospital, Sizzle approached me.

"Can I ask a personal question?" she asked.

"Of course you can, Sizzle."

"Do you freak?"

I looked at her. "No, I've never used drugs." In the biker world, someone "freaking" meant they were using LSD.

She laughed. "I meant, do you have sex with men?"

"Not to be disrespectful," I said, "but I have no interest in that."

Because I always treated people with respect, no matter their race, religion or sexuality, the "girls" gave me respect too, and days at work passed in a friendly and professional way. I spent a lot of time talking to two other guys living in my dorm at the end of my first week on the blue side, which is how I found out that Charlie Manson was at the California Medical Facility.

A couple of days later, I agreed to go and see what this notorious man looked like. His crimes had taken place while I was in high school so I hadn't really paid attention to the news. We found him working in the garden of the Catholic chapel – he was a small and unimpressive man, about five feet two inches tall, with wild hair and eyes and an unruly beard.

From what I know, Manson had been the figurehead of a group of people led by Charles "Tex" Watson to commit the murders of Sharon Tate and La Biancas. Before forming the Manson Family, he'd been a petty thief with no history of violence. He'd been friends with Doris Day's son, Terry Melcher, who he met through Dennis Wilson of the Beach Boys, while living at Wilson's house. He'd also tried to become a member of the Monkees, but lost that part to Davy Jones, and he stated many times that this rejection caused him to form the Family.

My actual interactions with Manson were limited to a couple of times when he came to the hospital clinic. It would be on these occasions that he would be trying to get pills for personal use, or to sell them on, as well as hyperdermic needles. I guessed these were for shooting up drugs. It would always follow the same pattern. First, he would try to be my friend. When that didn't work, he would offer me a bribe – drugs or money. With my continued unwillingness to help, he would resort to threats which, again, got him nowhere. This one time after I refused to give him what he wanted, he started shouting really loudly and acting crazy. He was out of control. Before we knew what was happening, a couple of Whites that were with him rummaged the nurses cart while everyone elase was trying to calm Charlie down.

He made the canteen the place where he would sell his autographs.

"Do you want one?" he asked me.

"Why?"

"Don't you know I'm famous?" he yelled. "I'll be more famous than even Jesus fucking Christ – you just wait and see!"

I would later hear that in September 1984 an inmate named Jan Holmstrom (who practised the Hari Krishna religion) got into an argument with Charlie over religion and doused him with paint thinner, before setting fire to his beard and face. Though he survived, this is what started Charlie on the road to protective custody, where he remained until he passed away on 19 November 2017.

I carried on with the orientation process, with physicals and psych appointments (common for a person serving a long sentence) to determine where I would be sent next. I was deemed to be a Level IV inmate so could go to one of two prisons, Folsom or San Quentin. There were only about 39,000 inmates in California at this time, spread out between the two prisons and 11 other institutions, fire camps and community centres. Folsom and San Quentin were the "Big Houses" – they were maximum security and had wardens, while all the other places had superintendents and housed inmates who were deemed to be lower status.

After about six weeks at the California Medical Facility, I was called out of my dorm at around 2:30am to report to surgery for an attempted suicide (something that happened at least three or four times every week). Part of my duties involved making a record of visible wounds, tattoos and scars for the doctor's official report. When I arrived, I realised this one had been successful.

When I went to view the body, I saw it was the guy who'd been my cellmate on the green side, the guy with 58 days to serve. He'd taken his own life with less than two weeks left until his release, by making a noose out of a sheet and lining it with razor blades. After tying it to the window and placing the noose around his neck, he jumped off the top bunk, severing his carotid artery and bleeding to death. I was sad to hear the guards joking about the 14-page "suicide note" he had left, explaining why his life wasn't worth living.

A couple of days later, I received notice that I was being sent to Folsom State Prison, though I had already heard the news. Sizzle and two of the other girls told me – they'd heard from the classification clerk. Apparently there had been an effort to arrange for me to stay at the California Medical Facility for my special skills but it had been unsuccessful.

My transfer happened in days.

12

Folsom State Prison

The morning I left to catch the bus was a strange one. The guys in the dorm were a bit standoffish with me, and only a few of them wished me luck at Folsom. Some of the guys had done time there and were grateful to be at the California Medical Facility, where there was much less violence, so I guessed there wasn't much luck to wish me.

We were again given a full strip search, which included having to show our assholes to a guard who seemed to enjoy the show, probably because it made him feel powerful. Once dressed, the guard ran a metal detector wand over us, before we were put in waist chains, handcuffs and leg chains. We then had to wait with about 30 to 40 other inmates who were all preparing to go to other institutions. When our names were called, the six of us going to Folsom were placed in the back of the bus, next to a guard in a cage with a 12-gauge shotgun and a gun port to shoot through.

This bus was painted in flat grey, which gave it the nickname "The Grey Goose". We had no seatbelts and I imagined the mayhem that would have occurred if the bus crashed. We left the same way we had arrived two months before: down to the sally port and out on to the main street, Alamo Drive, before heading east.

Our first destination was "Jamestown", officially called Sierra Conservation Center. It was one of two institutions called "fire camps" that trained inmates as fire fighters to help with the woodland wild fires that California suffers from every year. The other place was the California Conservation Center near the Nevada border, which was generally referred to as "Susanville".

After around half an hour, the main road started to wind into the western slopes of the Sierra Nevada mountains. As it was early summer, we could see a lot of greenery. This delighted a number of the guys heading to fire camp. Some had been there before and told the new guys what they could expect – better food, a dollar-an-hour pay for fighting fires and lots of fresh air. They said that when spring was greener, there would be more fires in the summer and autumn, so there would be more money to be made. Doing menial jobs around the camp only paid them about twenty cents an hour, so fighting fires was preferable – even though it put people and their houses in danger.

The trip went without any problems, and at some point we were joined by another bus behind us, until we finally stopped at a jumble of buildings. After a few minutes, a guard stepped aboard and said, "Alright gentlemen, whcn I call your names, stand up and exit the bus." He then called out around 20 names and, one by one, the men complied. They were placed against a wall and unshackled before being sent into a building. Once the last of the men had left the bus, the guard who had called their names followed them. Then the same happened with the other bus behind us and soon we were back on the road.

Jamestown to Folsom was an hour or so's journey until I saw the prison emerge from the landscape. Folsom State Prison is made from solid blocks of granite from the quarry inside it. Those housed here in the late 19th century put their blood into building this awful institution. We arrived at East Gate, which had the look of a medieval castle, with walls 26 feet high, a gun tower and huge solid gates. There was a feeling of despair in the air as the bus slowly rolled inside the first gate, which closed with such a solid clang that we could feel it in our souls. At the next set of gates we had to drive through, a sign above it said, "This is the End of the World."

After we cleared the gates, our guards gave up their weapons before we drove down a sloping road with buildings on the right. After one final turn we pulled up to West Gate, which led on to the prison yard. We stopped next to a concrete slab that said "R&R" above it – Folsom's Receiving and Release unit. The driver left the bus with an envelope of paperwork. There was a counter-like stand next to a gate marked "Five Count Gate".

Within minutes, a sergeant climbed on to the bus and told us to file off in an orderly manner and stand in a line. While our shackles were being removed, a dozen inmates were being led on to the bus. A few looked at us and shook their heads, aware of what awaited us. As I watched the bus drive away, a queen stood next me. Her name was Roxy and she'd hoped to avoid Folsom by doing the full girlie thing at the California Medical Facility – wearing eyeshadow, lipstick and nail polish, and performing oral sex. But apparently that hadn't worked, because here she was, with the rest of us desperadoes.

When the sergeant came back out, he pointed out the gun posts around the yard.

"At the first sign of trouble, guards have the right to shoot," he told us. "Each tower is manned by a 12-gauge shotgun, a mini-14 rifle and a 38 calibre pistol, and each guard is a crack shot." I would later learn that most guards failed to pass their shooting requirements on the first try, and most had to take it two or three times. "I want to welcome you all to Folsom State Prison," he said. "It was built in 1878 from the granite taken from the ground by men much like yourselves." He raised an eyebrow at Roxy. "We pride ourselves on having a well-run prison and won't tolerate violence."

As soon as these words left his mouth, a little Hispanic guy came out of Five Count Gate followed by a big guy holding a knife that was about 14 inches long. The little guy looked over his shoulder, and the guy with the knife caught up with him and stabbed him about half a dozen times before throwing down the knife and putting his hands up. The attacker was subdued by guards, handcuffed and led away. This was the second killing in prison that I'd witnessed.

Roxy had fainted from seeing all this. But the sergeant carried on as if nothing had happened. "As you can see, unscheduled things can happen at any given moment here at Folsom, so be careful and welcome to your new home." Then he turned to me and the guy on the other side of Roxy and said, "Pick up your girlfriend and go inside."

During processing, they explained that our clothing and bedding would have to last us a year and it was our responsibility to wash our own clothes, as there was no laundry for inmates. The guard called each of us in turn, asked our sizes in underwear, trousers, shirts, jackets and boots, and then two Hispanic inmates would scurry up and down the ladders and shelves, collecting the clothes. I noticed additional items on top of the clothes stack: four bandanas (two red, two blue), a screw-open razor with ten double-sided blades, a couple of pouches of tobacco, 20 packs of matches and a large kit of toiletries.

I asked the guard about the bandanas.

"It's so you can decide whose side you want to be on!" he said sarcastically. He then turned to his workers and laughed, before one of them led us to our cells.

When we arrived at the cells, the other inmates started to yell at us.

"Look – new fish!"

"Hey, can you smell the fear?"

"I want the bitch as my celly."

"None of you will get out of here alive."

"You've fucked up – you're in Folsom."

One by one we were each put in a cell, the barred door shutting with a clang and the heavy bolt that locked us inside dropping. After the last one of us was put away, the guard muttered under his voice, "A goddamn faggot – that's all I need."

Some of the others were already trying to find "homeboys" here at Folsom. "Homeboy" is to me a funny term. It's supposed to designate someone from your own neighbourhood, but in prison it often just means someone who's from your town or county or may have simply heard of where you're from. You may never have met this person before, yet now you were "homeboys" you were expected to be loyal to them and share everything without question.

People say the gangs in prisons were started to protect those from different races but that's not true. Those in white gangs manipulate and try to terrorise other whites but don't generally go after other races. It's the same with most of the race gangs in prison. But you'll find, from time to time, a small group of mates who watch each other's backs without trying to get involved in the politics of the prison yard.

I'd been in my cell for a couple of hours when a tall, blond-haired guy appeared on the other side of the bars.

"Hey homey, I hear you're from Fresno – whereabouts?" he asked.

I judged he was the sort of person I had no desire to get to know or hang around with. "Conas ta tu, cara, is mise Vannin," I responded which, in Gaelic, means, "How are you, friend? I am Manx".

Of course he understood none of it, so just stood there looking at me, before shouting down the tier to someone. "Are you sure this guy's white? He doesn't even speak English." He took one more look at me and then walked away.

I was living in a cell four feet by eight feet, with a toilet at the head of my bed. You might ask why would anyone sleep with their head towards the toilet and not the bars. The answer is that it's far better to have your feet cut or burned than your face. It wasn't uncommon for someone to throw lighter fluid (sold in the canteen) over a person through the bars before tossing a match in, or just reaching through the bars to try and slice a person's face or neck. There were even times when match bombs were thrown into a cell, so vigilance was important. There was no privacy, so it didn't matter if you were sitting on your bunk, on the toilet or sleeping – someone was always watching.

About three days later, a much bigger dark-haired guy showed up and started to engage me in conversation. I responded just as I had before but this guy didn't leave.

"You can cut that shit out," he said. "I know you can speak English, because some of the fellas heard you speaking to the guy in the cell above you."

After looking him up and down, I responded, "Yes I can speak English, but it's not my native tongue or my first language."

"Well, you're white aren't you?" he asked.

"No, I am a Celt," I said loudly.

I could see his brain was trying to wrap itself around what I'd said, but that something wasn't quite working for him.

"What's a Celt?" he said eventually.

I decided to explain in the simplest way I could, telling him that a Celt was where the roots of the Irish, Scots and Manx were and that I spoke Gaelic, their language. I thought this would have resolved everything but realised I may have only made things worse when he responded by saying, "I'm part-Irish."

In Fresno County Jail, I'd made a deliberate effort to do nothing that would keep me in prison any longer than the 13 years I'd been told I would serve. So I knew there were certain things I had to avoid, gangs being at the top of the list. But I did feel the need to point out that while this man was "part-Irish", he didn't know what a Celt was or recognise the

Irish language. He then wanted to know why I was listed as "Other" on my card and I told him that I'd been born on the Isle of Man. I showed him the words "Manx Bred" tattooed on my arms.

Clearly confused by our conversation, he started to leave but turned back to say, "Wesley wants to meet you when you hit the yard." He lumbered away.

For the seven days I spent on Orientation Row, we only came out to eat or take a shower. There were no meetings with counsellors or psychologists, and the only member of staff we saw besides the guards was the staff med nurse, who passed out medications every morning and evening to those who needed them. Finally, on the seventh day after breakfast, I found a paper on my bunk saying I was cleared to go to the yard and I would be moving to a mainline cell. It also gave me the name of my counsellor, the date of my classification meeting and how I could sign up to see the chaplain or for a medical.

I was moved to a cell on the third tier. As I had no celly, I took the bottom bunk. Once I'd stored my clothes and toiletries in the locker, I got ready to go out to the yard. However, my cell was soon unlocked and I was shouted to step out. I was worried that this "Wesley" character would be waiting for me. I had just cleared the gate on my cell block, when I saw two guys approaching me from either side, which put me on high alert. I gave each of them a look so they realised I knew they were there. The one on my right said that Wesley wanted to speak to me and they were just there to help me find him, for which I thanked them sarcastically.

They led me over to a stack of benches almost directly in front of Building 1, where it seemed that most of the white guys were gathered. I noticed a couple of older guys sat talking on the top bench, giving the impression they had no interest in me. Then a guy from the middle bench came down. I didn't feel threatened by him, as he was only a few inches taller than me but had a slighter build.

"I'm Wesley Tucker, and you're the confused guy who doesn't know he's white." He held out his hand for me to shake it, but I didn't take it.

"How do you know someone's white?" I asked him.

This caught him off guard and the older guys up on the bench turned to look at me.

"Because they say they are," he responded.

"I'm Manx. I'm a Celt. I'm not white. Nice to meet you." Then I walked away.

In all my years growing up, I never saw people as a colour. What I'd seen from my early childhood was that there are two types of people in the world: those who have and those who have not. I'd lived most of my life with the "have nots" But just because they didn't have material things, it certainly didn't mean they didn't love, laugh, cry and do the best they could for themselves and their children with what they did have.

In the centre of the yard, there was a track. It was very small and you weren't allowed to run on it – you could only walk slowly around it, counter clockwise. Guys did this for all their allotted yard time, talking in twos or threes, but there were some who talked only to themselves. The track had been built to be used in a movie called the *Jericho Mile* that had been filmed at Folsom in 1979 – this was about a lifer convicted of first-degree murder who could run a mile in less than four minutes and how the prison officials gave him the false hope that he could compete in the Olympics. It felt ironic given that over the next 34 years I would see lifers given false hope that they might be released, only to be denied this hundreds of times.

As I was trying to plan out how I would do my time, up walked Rico, the guy who lived above me. He was from Puerto Rico, though had been raised in New York and came to California to buy a large quantity of weed. The people selling it turned out to be undercover cops and gunfire erupted – when the smoke cleared, Rico had been wounded and a friend of his had been killed. Under California law, if there's a death as a result of a felony you committed, you can be convicted for it even if you played no role in the death. As a result, Rico was serving 15 years to life for a second-degree murder.

"The Others aren't sure why you're listed as an Other," he said to me.

"I was born on a small island in the Irish Sea," I explained

Rico told me that the Aryan Brotherhood (also known

as the AB) had approached the others about me – it seemed like I'd ruffled some feathers when I chose to walk away from Wesley. Rico told me to "watch my back".

For the next few days it seemed like I'd been forgotten. No one came to my cell or approached me on the yard except for a couple of Others, who asked me about my island. I could tell they were curious, so I engaged in a bit of conversation. On around my fourth day, I came back from morning chow to find a note on the floor of my cell saying I was being challenged to go to the "Smokers". This was a fight ring on the yard that allowed inmates to settle disputes with less bloodshed than a stabbing.

A little before yard time, Rico came to my cell with another guy, a Native American who called himself "Little Horse". When I told them I was going to fight Wesley, Little Horse said that I would probably be fighting someone else who could do me damage, likely one of the bigger "Woods". Wood was a shortened version of "Peckerwood", which started out as a derogatory term in the southern part of America and meant weak, poor or white trash, though in prison it was a source of pride.

When time came for yard call, I went out to meet my opponent. As I passed the building entrance, I could already see a large crowd of guys over by the Smokers, along with several guards. Wesley was standing in the middle of a crowd of about 20 whites, it sure seemed that he wanted to make sure I couldn't get to him. At this moment, I lost any respect I may have had for him.

One of the guards asked if I wanted to go through with it.

"Might as well – everyone wants a show," I replied.

I climbed into the ring. Another guard acting as referee gave me some thinly padded gloves – the type you would use on a speed bag and with which you could easily open up cuts on a man's face. I could hear the chatter around the outside of the ring, with people saying, "This guy's gonna get smashed." "He hasn't got a chance." "Who's he gonna fight?" and "What did he do?" I had to block it out so I could focus on what lay ahead.

When the voices quietened, I looked over at the guy entering the ring – it was the big guy who'd come to see me while I was on orientation row. He climbed in the ring with purpose and was given his gloves.

The guard brought us both into the middle.

"This isn't Marquis of Queensbury rules, so you'll fight until one of you can't get up," he said. "Is that understood?"

I took this as a warning that when I was knocked down I should stay down.

"I've got to hurt you, but I don't want to hurt you too much," the big guy said to me.

"Same to you," I replied.

As we turned to go back to our corners I knew that almost everyone had counted me out and that I was going to lose the fight. Then the bell rang and we approached the centre of the ring.

Just as we were within striking range, the big guy surprised me. "I'm going to allow you one hit, so take your best shot." He lifted his chin.

I immediately struck one in his throat and then kicked his knee. As he was dropping to the mat, I grabbed his head and slammed it as hard as I could into my knee, before letting him fall on to the mat unconscious. There was a deafening silence outside the ring and the inmates and guards watching looked stunned. People started to talk as I took off my gloves and the referee attended to my opponent, getting him out of the ring and on to a stretcher.

The people who'd seen the fight were suddenly talking over each other.

"What the hell happened?"

"Who is this guy?"

"Did anyone see what he did?"

"That's going to piss off Wesley."

That last comment really aggravated me. Who was this Wesley character to send someone else to fight his battles?

After I left the ring, I walked across the yard, hoping that whatever issue Wesley had with me would now be over. But I should have realised that the smallest men carry the biggest grudges, and I would soon find out that he wasn't done with me yet.

13

When I had been off orientation for over a week, it was time for me to go to my classification meeting to see what they wanted of me. I finally met my counsellor, who led me into a room where a captain, a sergeant and two other staff sat. My counsellor started to read out my conviction and the length of my sentence but then he stopped and looked at something in my file that had caught his eye. He took out a piece of paper and passed it to the other people at the table, who each looked at it. Finally the captain read it.

"So you were working as a surgical tech at CMF [California Medical Facility]," he asked.

"Yes, Sir", I replied.

"Would you be willing to be one here at Folsom?"

I told him I would. After a moment or two, it was agreed that I would report to the hospital that day. I felt pretty good, as I believed this job would keep me busy and all the other nonsense would just go away.

I reported to the hospital and was told to check in with the nurse at the desk in the surgery ward. As I walked up the stairs, I kept on thinking this job would fix everything. But then I saw Wesley Tucker talking to the nurse I'd been instructed to see.

The nurse and Wesley both looked in my direction. I don't know what look was on my face, but he looked as if someone had just pissed in his Cheerios.

"What are you doing here?" he asked.

I ignored him and handed the nurse the sheet from the classification committee. She looked at it and picked up the phone to make a call, speaking so quietly that I couldn't make out what she was saying. A moment after she hung up, a tall sandy-haired man in his 40s came out of an office, and called my name. It turned out he was a doctor and I'd been assigned to him. He told me that my counsellor had spoken to him and he was impressed by what he'd heard.

"We don't do major surgeries at Folsom," he explained. "But we do minor things like removing birdshot pellets from guys who've been shot, burning off offensive tattoos from inmates who are usually about to go on parole and removing cysts or lancing boils. But our most important task is stabilising anyone who has been stabbed, so they can be transported to an outside hospital."

He stood up, shook my hand and said one of the other guys working in the area would show me around. As we left his office, he called to Wesley.

Wesley's face reddened and there was a look of disdain in his eyes. But he led me down to a back room where three other guys stood.

"This guy Wetmore just snaked into the other surgical tech job without even discussing it with us," he said. "And you all know I'd planned on Reg getting that job when he got back from court. What do you think about that?"

The black and Hispanic guys started laughing and congratulated me, while the third guy, who was white, went to stand next to Wesley.

I turned towards him. "The name's Kane." I said in a blunt tone. "Wetmore was a slave name I was given by the people who bought me. Please don't tell me you're as stupid as the guard who processed me. But if you do want to see my Abstract of Judgement, come to my cell."

This just brought even more laughter from the other guys but Wesley gave me an angry look.

"Do you realise who I am? I'm Wesley Tucker from Orange County."

"And I'm Morgan James Kane and I'm from the Isle of Man."

"Well, I'm a lieutenant in the Aryan Brotherhood," Wesley responded.

"And I'm road captain for the Confederate Devils Motorcycle Club, so I guess that means I outrank you."

Unable to contain his anger, Wesley shouted out, "I've

had more than a dozen guys stabbed."

"Well that's the difference between us," I said in a soft tone. "I've shot more than a dozen men. So are you impressed? Because I'm not."

The guy behind Wesley grabbed him by the arm and said they needed to get out of there. Wesley left but not before giving me a hateful glance over his shoulder.

The two guys who'd been laughing came over and introduced themselves. One was a member of the Black Guerrilla Family, called Shakur, and the other was Marcos, a member of the Eme (Mexican Mafia).

"In my three years at Folsom, I've never seen anyone shut Wesley up like that," said Shakur, "but watch your back as he won't take it lightly."

"If I'd known how entertaining that was going to be, I'd have sold tickets," added Marcos.

They then showed me around.

I got back to my cell to learn that all hospital workers had to live in Building 3, as it was just outside the hospital door and we would need to be able to get there quickly in an emergency. I packed up my kit and moved to my new cell. I was relieved to learn that Wesley lived on the other side of the building and I was unlikely to encounter him, except at work.

The guy who lived to the right of me had his cell set up

in a very strange way. Instead of a bottom buck, he had a saddle rack, with a full size horse saddle. Once I was settled in, he asked how I was doing.

"I'm going to be working in the hospital so all is going to be good," I replied.

"Here are some things you're probably going to need, if the rumours are true." He passed me three phone books and a roll of duct tape through the bars. "You need to make a vest." He explained that I'd been the subject of considerable chatter, as people were trying to figure me out.

"You too?"

"I couldn't care less," he said. "I'm half-Filipino and half-Mexican and in ten years they haven't figured me out either. But your problem is that you look white but claim to be Other. I expect they'll be on you. A vest will give you a chance to survive a stabbing."

As I started to assemble a vest from the phone books, I asked him about the saddle. He said that a few years earlier he'd made one to sell in the prison store. After some bigwig from Sacramento bought it, suddenly more people, including guards, wanted his hand-built saddles so the staff allowed him to build them in his cell.

I'd been working in the hospital for about a week when I got word that Reg was back from court. He was mad that I'd taken the job he'd been promised by Wesley. He challenged me to the Smokers the next day. Reg was a brown belt in karate and was expected to wipe the floor with me. Rico and Little Horse came to me later that day.

"You ever fought anyone trained in karate," they asked.

I told them I hadn't.

"So you scared?"

"Being scared has no bearing on the outcome," I replied, "but we'll see what happens."

They wished me luck, but I still felt that whatever happened, I was on my own.

The next day I found myself back inside the ring, this time facing someone not much taller than me and certainly with less muscle than my last opponent. Reg didn't say anything to me before the fight, but looked like he had every intention to hurt me. Again, a lot of white guys were watching, hoping I'd get taught a lesson.

Standing in our corners waiting for the bell to ring Reg started doing all these karate moves, to the delight of the spectators. At the sound of the bell, we rushed towards each other. But at the last moment I dropped down on one knee and slammed my right hand into his groin as hard as I could. I held my left arm above my head to block any blows and he fell back, holding his crotch with both hands. There was silence all round.

I felt I needed to make it clear that I was tired of this, so I pulled Reg to his feet and slammed him on the ground, before leaving the ring again. I thought this would be enough to earn their respect for standing up for myself. They seemed to have sent their top contenders against me so I'd hoped they would just leave me alone.

This last fight made things in the hospital ward difficult though. The other workers started retelling the story every time Wesley was around and I noticed he was frequently absent from work, though the staff seemed not to notice.

I'd been at Folsom for almost three months and the threats seemed to die down. One day I had an appointment to burn off some Nazi tattoos, and this guy turned out to be one of the Aryan Brotherhood lot. I thought this was maybe a set up, so asked the guy why he wanted it done, to assess the situation. It turned out he had Jewish parents who wouldn't let him back home if he didn't have the tattoos removed.

"Are you Jewish too?" I asked him.

"No, I'm Aryan," he replied. "Only my parents are Jewish. They used to tell me about being children in the Nazi concentration camps and that they had numbers tattooed on their arms. But I don't believe all their propaganda."

"So why do you want to live with them then?"

"They're my parents and are getting old," he replied without a hint of hesitation.

There weren't many Jewish guys in prison in 1984, and it seemed strange to me that so many chose to align themselves with the white supremacists.

By the beginning of September, my job in the hospital

seemed to involve doing a lot more of the little things, such as taking books from the recovery ward and trading them for new ones. On one such round, I noticed Wesley and about eight other whites standing in my way. I knew that nothing good could come from this. As Wesley had been noticeably absent from the hospital in the last few months, I had a feeling that he'd been planning something – and I knew it wasn't going to be an apology.

As I approached the group Wesley asked if we could talk over by the yard fence, to which I agreed. I had about a dozen books in my hands and I'm sure he felt I would be at a disadvantage in a fight. The tower guard above us seemed to be paying no attention.

"Everyone is questioning my authority because you've disrespected me on many occasions," he said.

"I didn't start this thing between us," I replied. "I just want to be left alone."

He acted as if he hadn't heard me. "You have four choices: you can become my punk, you can become a mule, you can ask for protective custody or I can have you stuck. I hope you choose the first, as I need a new bitch."

I gave it a moment before answering. "I choose number five," I said quietly.

I dropped the books, giving him an uppercut. As he fell to the ground, the rest of the whites that were with him scattered. I picked him up, placed him on the fence and started hammering away at his stomach, aiming to knock all the air out of him. I was so mad he thought he could speak to me like that, I just lost it.

Suddenly a bullet hit the ground by our feet. I spun him off the fence just as another bullet hit where we'd been.

"Stop it – they're going to shoot us," he kept saying.

"What, are you afraid to die?" I replied.

Dozens of guards came running towards us so I let go of Wesley and put my hands up showing the guards I had no weapons. One guard who must have weighed about 300 pounds slammed into me and pushed me so hard against the fence that I had bruises on my back for weeks. They got us both face down on the yard and cuffed us.

We were placed in separate offices, and I could hear Wesley saying I was crazy. After about 10 minutes, a guy in a brown suit came in and looked me over real hard.

"Mr Wetmore, why have you felt the need to be so disruptive at my prison?" he asked. "I really don't like people who make waves and can't go along with the programme. Did I hear you say you weren't afraid to die?"

I looked him straight in the eye. "I just want to be left alone to do my time. I asked Wesley if he's afraid to die since he's the only problem I have. And I will 'hold my mud'." In the military, it meant not giving away any ground, but in prison I was learning it meant "don't tell on anyone".

I was sent to Administration Segregation (Ad Seg), while

they decided what charges to bring on me since I was seen as the aggressor in this incident. I wondered if I'd completely screwed up getting out in 13 years. I had no idea what to do, but all alone in a cell you have lots of time to think.

I was taken to a classification hearing two days later and was told I was being given a write-up for simple assault, as I'd done no permanent harm to anyone. This was going to cost me 90 days of good time credits and I was recommended for transfer to another prison. They believed Wesley Tucker and I had issues with one another that were not going to be resolved and they belelieved, in this instance, that he was the victim. They told me my next detention would be San Quentin. Little did I know I'd be heading there the next morning.

14

San Quentin State Prison

The guard shone a light into my eyes to wake me. It was 3am. He told me to get dressed and come up to the bars, turn around and stick my hands behind me. I felt the cold bite of the metal cuffs clicking around my wrists. He instructed me to step forward into my cell but not to turn around, at which point he opened the door and pulled me out. We headed to the stairwell and down to the first tier, him pushing and shoving me all the way.

Finally we left the building and walked out to the yard where I could see a parked van. It was a dark night, though the lights shining from the buildings meant I couldn't see any stars. I was shoved into the van and the guard pulled the seat belt across my lap so tightly that it felt as though he was cutting off circulation to my legs. Then he slid in next to me and shut the door. This was the most uncomfortable two-hour ride of my life. By the time we reached San Quentin, my hands and legs were numb. The guard pushed me out of the van and

I fell to the ground. I couldn't stand up on my own so two inmates had to help carry me inside.

I was dumped on a bench and left for about 10 minutes before a guard came to take my chains off. I could finally rub some feeling back into my hands and legs. The guard who had ridden with me from Folsom gave me a half smile as he left, as if he knew some secret I didn't.

After nearly an hour of waiting, an inmate called me up to the counter, so I had a chance to take in my surroundings. Four inmates were moving around, while two guards sat drinking coffee. The guards were changing shift, and I could tell by the glances in my direction that information about me was being passed on.

Finally one of the guards came over.

"Word of what happened at Folsom has probably already reached here, so you need to watch your back," he said to me, leaning in close.

To get from the lower yard to the upper yard, there was a long, narrow set of stairs. I was nervous walking up them as there was no railing on one side; carrying an armful of clothes and bedding while trying to balance was no easy task. I pushed my right shoulder against the wall and crept up slowly. All the while, the guard was telling me about the layout of San Quentin. The upper yard contained all the housing units (including death row), as well as the administration buildings, medical clinics and wards, chapels, main canteen, library, education classes and chow halls. The lower yard contained the exercise areas, gymnasium, a small canteen, a Native American sweat lodge, the Receiving and Release unit (R&R) and the work change gate for those working in the industrial shops.

San Quentin was apparently the oldest prison in California. In 1851, a 268-ton wooden ship named the Waban anchored in San Francisco Bay and was outfitted to house 30 inmates. After a series of speculative land transactions, the ship's inmates built San Quentin and it opened the following year, with 68 inmates. The dungeon built at San Quentin in 1854 is thought to be California's oldest surviving public work and was still in use when I arrived. The prison held male and female inmates until 1932, when a women's prison was built at Tehachapi.

As we reached the housing units I heard a loud call from behind me "dead man walking" I assumed it was a threat against me and a shiver ran through me. The guard suddenly stopped and told me to face the wall. I heard chains rattling behind me. Out of the corner of my eye, I could see a guy covered in chains being escorted by three guards. There was a gun walk above us and a gunner with his rifle aimed at him. This was clearly a death row inmate being escorted. I wondered whether all this was necessary.

Since that day, every time I heard "dead man walking", I would get a feeling of dread. I'd hear it whenever other inmates were in the area, because it was a warning call. I later learnt it was also used to prevent anyone from attacking the chained inmate. Once the escort was out of sight, the guard told me to move along.

"Welcome to your new home," he said as he led me through an archway with two signs: "South Block" on the left and "Alpine Section" on the right. In the middle, there was a podium where a couple of guards were standing. "I've got a new one for you," he said to them before he turned to leave.

The two guards told me to stand against the wall whilst they continued to talk quietly among themselves. I looked at the first tier of five and was surprised to see an inmate sitting in a reclining armchair, wearing a leather vest and a black cowboy hat. He was petting a cat on his lap and gently talking to it.

"Hey Rory, take this fish up to his cell," one of the guards hollered.

The guy gently put down his cat and walked over to collect a piece of paper from the guards. Then he waved at me to follow him.

As we reached the third tier he led me to an empty cell and told me to stand up against the wall. Then I heard the bar crack and all the cell doors opened and inmates poured through them. We'd arrived at a time when all the inmates with job assignments were going off to work. Once the tier had cleared Rory opened my cell door, put down the stuff he had been carrying and told me to get settled in.

"Thanks," I said. "So, you're Rory?"

"No, it's just because of the cowboy hat," he said. " Some of the guards said I look like a Western star called Rory Calhoun, and the nickname has just stuck. See you around."

At noon, a guard passed me a boxed lunch through the bars, and told me I would be going to classification at 3pm. By the time I was called, I'd made my bunk and put my property away.

Once I got to the classification room I found a couple of guys waiting, neither looking happy. I assumed they'd been there for ages and were fed up of waiting, so I was surprised to be called next. The committee was made up of counsellors, a captain, someone representing education and another person who represented the prison industries. They asked me to sit down at the head of the table.

"We know you worked as a surgical tech at your last two institutions, but we don't have that position here at San Quentin," the captain said to me. "If you're interested in working in the hospital you can be a ward aide. You'll be changing hospital bedding and generally helping out the medical staff. Would this work for you, or would you prefer a different assignment?"

"Happy with that Captain and I'll do my best," I replied.

"Then you'll receive an assignment ducat tonight," he said. "And you'll report for work in the morning."

At about 5pm we were sent down for the evening chow. This was my first look at the San Quentin chow hall. It was a bit smaller than the ones at Folsom. The only sound you could hear was the scraping of metal utensils against metal trays along with the occasional soft whisper among inmates. What really caught my attention were the guards on the gun walks high above our heads – one of them carried a rifle and the other had a block gun. A block gun fired a 40-millimetre wooden block that would shatter into pieces of jagged wood when it hit a stone wall or floor – capable of ripping into human flesh.

The next morning, as I reported for my hospital job at 6.30am, I was pleased no inmates seemed to notice I was a new guy. The senior nurse ran through my duties. I happily spent the day changing bedding, helping to feed sick inmates and was even asked to read to one inmate who'd become blind through diabetes. Just before the end of my shift, the same senior nurse asked me to go and see Rory in my unit. He was going to give me something to bring back to her the next day. Arriving back, I asked the guard where I might find Rory.

"If he's not in his recliner, he'll be in his cell – first one on the left," he replied.

Rory was sitting on his bed in a robe and slippers, with a crocheted blanket over his bunk, reading a book. What surprised me most was that he had a fish tank on a table and above his bed there was a stained glass lampshade hanging from a chain. Rory told me to come back the next morning before I went to work.

The following morning, Rory was sitting in his recliner outside his cell. He got up when he saw me this time and went into his cell, returning with a canvas bag. Handing it over, he told me to be very careful because the contents were fragile. Inside the bag, I saw five little kittens, softly mewing.

"Don't worry," he said, "She knows what to do. Now off with you, before they shut the doors for the work line."

I joined the mass of moving inmates and made my way to the hospital. When the nurse saw the bag, her eyes lit up. She took it and hurried off, leaving me very confused.

The next few days were a perfect routine. Finally I felt I would be able to do my time, stay out of trouble and focus on getting home. It was all I wanted for my family in the first place. However, I hadn't received a single letter from Amy since I'd been in prison. Then, three or four days after I delivered the kittens to the nurse, she called me into her office. There, in a cardboard box lined with blankets, were the kittens.

"Can you take them back to Rory," she asked.

"I thought you were taking them from the prison," I replied, astounded.

"No, my husband is a veterinarian. I took the kittens to give them a check and their shots."

I learned that a couple of guys had females that they bred, but to keep down the population most of the kittens were spayed or neutered. After work I delivered the precious cargo back to Rory. He was happy to see me, and told me the mother had been restless while her kittens were gone.

Going back to my cell I saw a guy standing outside my cell, with his face pressed against the bars. When I was within a few feet of him he must have heard my footsteps as he started to turn away.

"See anything interesting?" I asked.

He muttered something about trying to toss a message on my bunk.

"What does the message say?"

"Read it yourself," he said in an agitated tone.

He tried to walk away but I grabbed him and pushed him back. In response, he pulled a sharpened piece of metal on me. It was about seven inches long and as thick as a pencil.

"Let me go or people won't be happy as I'm just the messenger," he said, holding the metal in his left hand.

"I asked you, 'What's in the note?'," I said.

Again, he said I needed to read it, before trying to get past.

With a quick spin, I struck the back of his hand. The weapon fell over the side, making a small clanking sound as it hit the main floor three storeys below. He landed against the railing bars and, with a stern glance at me, slithered past and ran for the stairs. The gunner was just making his turn on to the gun walk across from where I was standing. I wondered whether he would have shot us if he'd been there just a moment or two before.

Back in my cell I retrieved the note from under my bed. Sitting up on my bunk I opened the sealed envelope. In the crudest writing I'd ever seen the note said, "Haye Punx, yo aske its bigg treble. Dounut bee own yord morrie. Weve rar whinting fo yoo." It was signed with crosses, I assumed knives. This had to be a threat – a warning that I shouldn't be on the yard the following morning – so naturally I decided to go there. I liked surprises and hoped they did too.

On my way back from breakfast the next morning, I stopped by Rory's to ask if he had any spare newspapers. He had a whole stack of them on his bed. With a smile on his face, he reached into his cell and handed them to me – along with a roll of masking tape.

"By the way, there are two *National Geographic* magazines in the middle of the stack that you might find useful," he said as I was turning to leave.

I made my way back up to my cell, and taped multiple layers of newspapers around my calves and a *National Geographic* to each forearm. Then I taped an inch and a half of newspaper to the inside of the back of my denim jacket. I laced up my boots and put on my denim jacket and woollen pea coat. Lastly I donned my woollen cap and weightlifting gloves, just before the cell doors were opened for yard call.

As I headed out of the building, I paid extra attention to those walking out to the yard with me. It seemed a lot of eyes were focused on me. I reached the lower yard by going via those narrow steps with no rail. It felt like the perfect place for a trap. I started walking slow laps of the yard while taking in what was going on around me. I kept a particular eye on the weight pile area, as I noticed a number of white boys over there stopping and staring every time I passed. After about an hour of walking, I decided to sit down on one of the sets of bleachers as it gave me a good view of the yard. Then a guy approached me and called me by my name. It took me a moment to realise who he was – he had been in the "High Power" section at Fresno County Jail with me, a guy named Jericho. He'd been in a cell across from mine in Fresno, and knew me from my friendship with the Stankewitz brothers, who were from his reservation. The younger Stankewitz brother, Dougie, was on death row at San Quentin and had the misfortune of being the first inmate to be put on there after the death penalty had been reinstated in 1978.

Jericho told me the Whites had been enquiring if I was running with the Native Americans and Islanders. They'd said no, which automatically meant I couldn't go to them for help. As usual I was on my own. But Jericho reassured me that if he or any of the Natives heard anything about me, they would at least give me heads up.

"Appreciate it," I said. "I got a note from someone. If they want to mix it up with me, I'll be very happy to."

He laughed. "I don't think they're ready for a storm, Sunrise." Then he walked back to the sweat lodge next to the track with some other Native Americans.

I waited until noon and nothing happened. The next day, I got myself "suited and booted" and repeated the previous day's activities, but still no move on me.

During the next week I was busy with my job, having been asked to work extra hours as lots of inmates were in the ward. Though I would see Rory a couple of times each day, I didn't ask him if he'd heard anything from the Whites, nor did I share the note with him. I figured he already knew everything that was going on.

On Saturday, I wondered if they may think I'd let my guard down by now. As well as my usual protection, I also rolled up a magazine as tightly as possible into a strong and durable baton, which I concealed up my jacket sleeve. It was completely undetectable, yet I could drop it into my hand just by opening my fist. I was ready for another day on the yard.

I tried to stay aware of those around me, as I had the previous weekend. I made my way to the lower yard and started to walk some laps of the track at a slower pace, anticipating that something was about to happen. I wanted this situation done and dusted – I hated having to always look over my shoulder. Finally I sat on the bleachers and leaned back as if I was relaxing. Within a couple of minutes, I saw a couple of the Native Americans walking behind me.

"Twelve and nine," one of them said in a low voice as they passed me. No one more than a foot away could have heard, and they didn't break stride.

Looking out across the yard, I saw two guys looking like they were standing by themselves, smoking cigarettes. I climbed down from the bleachers and headed for the mini canteen, where we could buy coffee, ice cream, candy and sodas. I'd decided I would try to control the situation, and there were some blind spots by the canteen.

Almost straight away, the smoking guy began to move in a parallel direction at a slightly quicker pace, though when I looked for the other guy he was nowhere to be seen. I ordered a cup of coffee. As soon as the words were out of my mouth, the other guy punched me on the left side of my face. I was a bit stunned but dropped the baton into my hand and used it to block the knife in his left hand. I then pushed his hand back towards him and he slashed open his own face between his nose and cheek. He dropped the knife with a yelp and disappeared around the side of the canteen. Turning around I kept my back to the building. Out of nowhere, I became aware of the other guy who was arcing a knife towards me. I was just able to bring my left arm up in time to block him, only to have the knife go straight into my forearm. I struck his wrist with my baton, causing him to let go of the knife and jab it into his own eye. He then retreated, cursing.

I pulled the knife from my forearm − as I felt no pain I assumed it must have been stopped by the *National Geographic* I'd taped there. I threw the knife down one of the drains as I didn't want to be caught with it. I calmly took my coffee from the canteen and went back to the bleachers, to wait for yard recall. I didn't even think about the first guy's knife, though I later heard one of the Natives had picked it up – a "good knife" was nice to have on most prison yards. No alarms were raised for the guy with the sliced cheek. So I figured some guys must have helped to clean his wound and patch him up, but I knew he would need stitches. Finally the yard call came and it was time for me to return to my cell.

When I removed my "armour" from my left forearm, I discovered the knife had only slightly penetrated the skin. It would have been much worse if I hadn't been so prepared: if I'd been hit in the back, I would have been killed. Now I knew the two by sight, they would be on the defensive – and they knew it.

Just as I was assessing how it all went, Rory appeared at the bars of my cell, holding one of the kittens. "Now that you don't have anything to preoccupy yourself, would you like her?"

I started telling him that I'd never been a cat person.

"This is the runt of the litter, about half the size of the others," he said. "Figure she'll have her best chance with you – since you've been in the medical corps. I usually sell my kittens for a carton of cigarettes, but no one would pay that for this runt. She'll get used to you in time."

He put his hand through the bars and placed the kitten in my hands. Then said he'd be back later with a few things for her. Not being someone with a great imagination for naming animals, I called her "Kayt", which is Gaelic for cat. True to his word, just before lights out that night, Rory brought me some cat food, a couple of small blankets, a plastic pan to use as a litter tray and a plastic ball with a bell inside. I guess I had a new cellmate.

At work the next week, I read the report on the guy with the sliced face. He couldn't say who'd done it to him so had been locked up for his own protection and would be sent to another institution, most likely Folsom. I took Kayt to work with me because I was worried about leaving her alone. The senior nurse gave me a small bottle and some cat vitamins so I could develop her immune system and told me to bring her to work whenever I liked.

Around two months later, I heard the shout "dead man walking" at the main canteen. Those of us in the canteen line had to sit on the ground, to ensure no one would try to attack the inmate. This time I could actually see the person. It was Dougie Stankewitz. I heard the guard say he was going to the clinic, so I took my canteen purchases back to my cell and headed to work.

By the time I arrived, Dougie was in the treatment area having a bandage changed. I approached one of the guards who were escorting him. He asked what I wanted.

"I'm Jamie," I replied. "I'm friends with Dougie, and Johnnie, and wondered if I could speak to him."

"Wait here."

I thought he was going to call for the other guards, but a moment later he said, "Don't let me see you talking to him," and walked to the end of the corridor. I opened the curtain and saw Dougie up close for the first time in about 10 years.

"You haven't changed much," he said to me when he looked up. "Nothing personal against you but I've no use for Whites, after all they've done to my people. So just leave."

I did just that but felt sad – this wasn't the boy I'd known who was always laughing, instead this was a man with the burden of his nation on his shoulders.

I'd heard that once the attempt on my life had failed yet again, Rory had used some of his influence to tell people to leave me alone. He wasn't a "shot caller" but with the years he'd served and the number of murders he'd arranged, he was given a great amount of respect. Of course I also had one of his kittens and he liked to check that she was being treated well. Kayt used to sleep across my throat and purr, which was such a strange sensation – though I think it was the fact that she occasionally used my bare back as a scratching post when I was asleep that really bonded us. It was probably also something to do with the fact that on Friday nights the chow hall served us whole fish and I would take bits back to the cell for us to share. Life for the next five months wasn't too bad.

On my first Christmas in prison, I was woken at 4:30am by

a guard setting down a small paper bag outside every cell. These bags were put together by volunteers and given out every year. They served us Christmas dinner – so much food that it needed two trays. We were each given a huge slice of turkey breast, a slice of ham, mash potatoes and gravy, yams, green beans with almonds, cranberry sauce, salad, two buttered rolls and a piece of pumpkin pie with whipped cream and ice cream. We received this kind of holiday meal for a while, but as the prison population rose, the quality and quantity of the food fell.

Coming back to my cell one day after work in March 1985, I couldn't find Kayt. Cats would often go out through holes at the back of the cells, but she had never done that before. Within minutes of all the inmates being locked up, I could hear guys asking if anyone had seen their cats. I had a sick feeling in my stomach. Then a sergeant came to the top of the stairs and made an announcement.

"Gentlemen, all the cats have been removed by an administration order from the warden, due to a complaint regarding health and safety," he shouted. The inmates started shouting obscenities at him, and he waited for a minute before going on. "Please do not stab any member of the prison staff, as they didn't want to do this. If you must take it out on someone, take it up with the inmate in cell number 420, as he was the one who made the complaint."

With that, the sergeant went back down stairs and sure enough, the guy in cell 420 began to get death threats. I suddenly wondered how Rory was coping. He'd had his cat for eight years and her mother for about 10 years before that. What was he going through? Right after the guards' shift change, the guy in cell 420 began telling the gunner he needed to see the prison lieutenant. It took about an hour for guards with riot shields to come get him. As he was being walked off the tier, inmates threw cans of food and glass jars of piss at him. From then on, there was nowhere he would be safe.

Less than a week later, we heard there had been a large riot at "Gladiator School". This was another name for Deuel Vocational Institution, which had been originally built for juveniles and was generally for 18 to 26-year-old prisoners. Because of this incident, 500 of the youngsters were being brought to San Quentin, and 500 of the older guys from here would be shipped to Deuel Vocational Institution, in the hope that they could get the youngsters to toe the line. I'd only been in the prison system for a year, but being over 30 meant I was selected to go. Knowing I was going to a place of young, stupid guys where there had just been a major riot didn't sit well with me – it felt like the powers that be were trying to put me in situations where getting home in 13 years wouldn't be possible.

Two days later, I was on a convoy of buses to make the switch. The mood was foul to say the least. "We weren't sentenced to be goddamn babysitters," many guys muttered.

15

Deuel Vocational Institution (DVI)

I knew little about Deuel Vocational Institution, other than it was for younger guys who were too violent for the California Youth Authority system. I also knew it was the most unstable of all the correctional facilities in California. Deuel Vocational Institution is located in San Joaquin Valley near the town of Tracy, halfway between Fresno and Sacramento. It was opened in 1953. In 1956, the Mexican Mafia gained influence there and within a short time, Deuel Vocational Institution became full of youths who were too violent for youth facilities. Because of this violence it gained the nickname "Gladiator School". The running joke on the bus was we would be issued with a sword and a trash can lid to use as a shield. On arrival we were placed in the Receiving and Release holding tanks to await processing. The plan was to load up the youngsters going to San Quentin first, so we were told to relax. A lot of the guys stood at the bars to see if they knew anyone, but I was sure there would be no one from my past here.

A group of 10 shackled guys walked past our tank to get on the bus, with one guard leading them. When a second group of 10 was next to our tank, all four of the clerks from behind the counter came over and started stabbing some of the chained-up guys. When your legs are held with three-feet chains and there's a chain connecting your waist to the handcuffs and keeping your arms at your side, there's no way you can defend yourself. This attack was so vicious that guys closest to the bars were sprayed with blood. Within less than two minutes, five guys were bleeding on the floor, and the four assailants were being restrained by guards. As the assailants were lifted from the floor, soaked in their victims' blood, they were still swearing at and spitting on their victims.

All I could think about was how I was going to get through this. The four attackers were Hispanic and the five who had been stabbed were White, and I "looked white", so if this was an on-going war, it wasn't likely that anyone would ask me "what I was" before trying to stab me.

The guys covered in blood were trying to get to the only sink to clean their faces and mouths, the victims' blood was coagulating on the floor. It took about five minutes for any medical staff to arrive, place the victims on gurneys and roll them away. At least two of the victims were already dead and I thought it was very likely that they'd all die. Finally, with the attackers sent to Ad Seg, the victims to medical clinic and their blood still on the floor, the prisoners going to San Quentin were finally loaded on the bus.

After the bus pulled out, one of the guards asked for some volunteers to help clean up the blood. Three men set about their task with some rags, a mop and a bucket, while the rest of us were called out one at a time to be interviewed about our housing. When my interviewer came to the section on my papers where it said race and stated "Other", he raised an eyebrow.

"So why are you "Other?" he asked.

"I'm Manx."

After a couple of moments, they finally looked at me. "Good luck – you're going to have a hard road here," he said, in almost a whisper.

Walking back to the tank, I gained a better idea of the severity of the attack. Blood had sprayed all the way to the ceiling and the guys cleaning up were standing on a rickety stepladder trying to reach it. With most of us processed, we were taken to our cells – the next bus from San Quentin was due to arrive and they needed the room for the next group.

Deuel Vocational Institution had been built in a similar design as Vacaville: a long corridor led to housing units, and another corridor led to the chow halls, workshops, education classes, medical department and other offices. As we came to each unit, one or two guys were dropped off. Once we were 100 feet from the end of the corridor I was finally inside C Wing, with my bedroll in one hand and some papers to give to the housing officer in the other. I could hear conversations between the cells –so many people were talking, it was like being in a beehive. Finally the housing officer came over to ask me for my paperwork and took me to a ground floor cell – 110. He told me my cellmate was a guy named Pietro who was a bit strange, and then had the other guard open the cell door before closing it behind me. Unlike the doors at Folsom and San Quentin, these ones were solid, with glass windows for the guards to look through. There was also a large window in the back of the cell that could open about six inches, and around it were small fixed windows. My cellmate wasn't there and the top bunk was empty, so I made my bed, put away my things and went to sleep.

About six hours later, the cell door slammed open and shut. I woke at the first sound but didn't jump up as I didn't want to start something with my cellmate. Pietro walked to the back of the cell, and muttering something like a prayer, sat down on his bed and started to roll a cigarette. As he was lighting it, I came down from my bunk and looked at him. He looked about 60, which surprised me. I thought Deuel Vocational Institution was generally for much younger guys. He was around five feet seven inches with a slim build.

I introduced myself.

He looked at me and tried to size me up. "Are you White or Other?" he asked in a heavy Italian accent.

"I'm listed as Other," I responded.

"Well it will depend on whether Pineapple will let you in the Others' 'Car'," he said after a few draws on his cigarette. I knew if Pineapple did accept me, this meant I'd have the support of their group. "My last name is Pietro, but call me 'Pie Man' as I work in the bakery."

Pineapple wouldn't accept Pie Man as an Other, so he'd been trying for months to be accepted by the Whites, at least until this most recent riot. As we talked I learnt he was actually from Rome but had been brought to America by his parents when he was 10. He was now just 24 but had started doing drugs at 11 and had been imprisoned off and on since he was 12.

Within days of my arrival I was assigned to work in the medical clinic which by now, didn't surprise me. My duties were mainly to change the bandages of those who'd been stabbed or cut in fights, almost a daily occurrence there. In fact, stabbings and killings were so common that staff in the clinic had a board where they would place bets on how many would happen each month. Life was seen as so cheap, and violence was so prevalent, that staff didn't seem to care who died, as long as they weren't put at risk. Guards around the prisoners were only given a whistle and a pair of handcuffs, and most carried a flashlight that they occasionally used as a makeshift baton. The only real batons were made of wood.

These were kept locked up in the Watch Office; to check one out in an emergency, a guard had to exchange a brass token. But by the time they'd done that, the incident would generally be over. So most guards relied on the manned hall gun posts when tensions among prison groups were running high, as well as on the gun towers on the yard. The gun towers had six gunners, armed with mini-14 semi-automatic rifles. Unfortunately the gunners weren't always good shots, and a random prisoner who wasn't even involved in a fight might be shot accidentally, even when they were yards away. If an alarm was set off, prisoners were required to lie flat on their stomach, wherever they were. To hesitate or try to move somewhere more comfortable could result in being shot.

I treated survivors of the shootings once they were stable enough to be brought back from an outside hospital. I thought 1985 seemed an especially bad year for prisoner injuries. But when I looked back through some of the hospital logs, I realised many other years had been far worse. Some cells in the clinic were fitted with concrete bunks and nothing else; these were for inmates with extreme mental health issues. The guards would put an inmate in there completely naked and give them a single blanket at night, which they would remove at about six in the morning. These cells were kept at a low temperature to keep the prisoners calm. The mental health staff consisted of one psychiatrist, who would show up once or twice each week with Bourbon on his breath. His most common solution was to medicate the inmates with Thorazine or Prolixin, which was often referred to as a "liquid lobotomy" because prolonged use could cause permanent damage to brain cells. The daily care for inmates with mental health issues was otherwise handled by a nurse and a psychology student.

I don't know what made me ask the senior medical staff in the clinic if I could check on the patients held in the zombie cells, but amazingly I was given permission, not only to do hourly checks but also to give them warm coffee and sit outside their cells to talk to them, if I wished. I was warned that my kind gestures would probably not be well received and I was told to expect to be spat on and cussed at. The men in these cells were thought to be hopeless, and the staff referred to them as "animals".

When I introduced myself to these inmates, I explained in a calm-but-firm voice that I would be bringing coffee and was willing to listen to whatever they had to say. Though I couldn't promise I could do anything, I wanted them to know I actually cared about how they were being treated. I told them if they threw coffee on me or became unruly, the staff wouldn't allow me to come back, so it was up to them how this went. At no time did I ever experience a problem, and even the other staff noticed the inmates were calmer and more stable. About a month later, I was able to get the chief medical officer to order that they be allowed boxer shorts to give them some dignity.

During the first three months of being in a cell with Pie Man, he would regularly ask me to bring back pills and needles from the clinic – for his use as well as for the inmates he was trying to be accepted by. I explained that I wouldn't do anything that might extend my sentence, as I was hoping to get back to my family. This thoroughly disappointed him. I realised we would never be mates; the fact that our work hours made it easy to avoid interactions with him was a blessing. He worked from 2am until 10am and I often worked from 8am until 10pm, as I was the only orderly for the clinic. On many occasions, I returned to our cell and could see by the evidence left on the table that he'd been doing drugs.

I used my free time to work out with weights, both in the clinic and in the gym. I chose not to go out to the yard since I didn't run with any Car and anyway, that's where the most serious violent incidents happened. I was lucky not to have to go to the chow hall, as the clinic had its own kitchen where I could get meals – the chow hall was the second most dangerous spot for stabbings. Since I had so little time when I wasn't at work or in my cell, I didn't feel the need to mix with other inmates. The incidents at Folsom and San Quentin didn't seem to have followed me, which gave me a bit of a reprieve from having to be constantly on my guard.

I struck up an acquaintance with one black guy who was a bit of a loner. We would often spot for each other when we were lifting weights; he could lift more than 300 pounds, and with his encouragement I got up to 275 pounds without much problem. One day he told me that I should try to get accepted into the "300lb Club", which had a very exclusive set of weights on the yard. Anyone was allowed to try for membership. After a week or so, I was finally able to bench press 310 pounds five times in a row – for membership of the 300lb Club, you had to be able to bench press 300 pounds ten times in a row. I wasn't completely sure I could do it, but I asked for the chance to try. My request was accepted and I was given a date for my trial, in front of all the other members.

The group of men all looked quite impressive, with chests ranging from 54 to over 60 inches and biceps between 22 and 26 inches in circumference. The guy who held the record for lifting almost 600 pounds would be my spotter. When I sat down on the bench, the coach asked me what I was. I responded, "I'm an Islander." He marked that down on the paper and told me to give him a sign when I was ready, at which point my spotter would allow me to start my routine. I could see the men around me looked unsure about my chances of success, which added to my determination.

I finally announced to the coach that I was ready, and the guy who was spotting for me, Iron Mike, lifted the 300-pound bar off the bench rack and placed it in my outstretched hands. With what seemed like the whole world watching, I started pounding out the reps and I could hear the group counting them out. By the time I had done the eighth rep, my shoulders and arms were burning. Though I realised I would make it to 10, something inside me drove me on until I hit my 15th rep. Only then did I allow Iron Mike to take the bar from me.

Though most of the guys congratulated me and welcomed me to the club, I noticed a few guys giving me angry looks as the coach presented me with my new card. About a week later, these guys approached me while I was working out in the gym. It turned out that Pineapple, leader of the Islanders' Car, was also the leader of their group. Pineapple explained that he was half-Samoan and half-Maori and that in no way was I an Islander. To anyone viewing this little interaction, the differences between us would have been obvious. I was five feet six inches, 175 pounds with a 50-inch chest and 18-inch biceps. He, on the other hand, was about five feet ten inches tall, 265 pounds with a 60-inch chest and 24-inch biceps. I knew if this became physical, I would have to get him before he got me. I tried to explain where I was from and that I was indeed an Islander, at which point he made a few derogatory comments about the British Isles and said that if I ever called myself an Islander again, he would smash me.

I wasn't going to listen to anybody trying to dismiss my heritage. So when he was turning away from me, I called to him and slammed my left fist into the right side of his jaw. To my surprise, though I heard bones snapping, I'd only knocked him back by about two feet. He grabbed me by my shirt, lifted me above his head and slammed me to the ground, before repeating the same action four more times. I found myself lying on the mat feeling bruised and battered, with a terrible throbbing in my left hand. Looking up, I saw him rubbing his face and muttering something about a broken jaw. I somehow dragged myself up to face him again, though my legs were wobbly. With every ounce of energy I could muster, I punched him with my right hand, which he wasn't expecting. It brought extreme pain to my right hand as well, and I heard more bones cracking. He staggered back by about a foot, before grabbing me by my chest, lifting me off the ground and throwing me about four feet into the brick wall behind me. I bounced off the wall and landed on my face, after which he picked me up and threw me down more than a dozen times. The two guys with him were patting him on the back.

"I'm not done with you yet," I called out to Pineapple as they were walking away.

"Well, I'm done with you," he replied as he left the gym.

As I was lying there, the black guy I worked out with came over and helped me sit up. He gave me some water and told me that this was the stupidest thing he'd ever seen anyone do in prison. After he'd helped me to my feet, I headed off to the medical clinic as it was almost time for work and I was desperate to have a shower.

Noticing my hands were swollen, I told the nurse that I'd banged them on dumbbells while I was working out. As

I went in to X-ray, Pineapple was just coming out. She told the inmate X-ray technician to X-ray my hands as I'd had a weight-pile injury, to which he responded, "That's the second one I've had today," while giving me a smirk.

When I went back into the clinic, Pineapple was sitting two tables away. It turned out I'd broken his jaw in three places, and he'd lost one tooth. I'd fractured my left hand and a few knuckles on my right hand. I ended up with a cast on my left hand, while Pineapple had to go to an outside hospital to have his jaw wired.

It was more than a week before I saw Pineapple again. Realising he was at the clinic to get puréed meals because he couldn't eat solid food, I snuck him a gallon of ice cream from the ward kitchen and apologised. He made a noise that sounded like "Fuck you, Island Man" in response but gave me a thumbs up, before walking away. For about three weeks I had bruises on my shoulders, back and chest, which gave me time to reflect on the risk of underestimating an opponent and allowing myself to get goaded into responding.

About a month later, a couple of guys in the Islander Car told me that Pineapple wanted to see me. It turned out it was his birthday. Though he couldn't eat a lot of solid foods, it was traditional among the Car to do something similar to a Luau (a feast).

"Join us," he said. "I can't speak for every Islander in the prison system, but the ones here at DVI [Deuel Vocational

Institution] will let you call yourself an Islander. You're not very smart, not that tough and certainly not strong enough, but at least you have the determination Islanders are known for."

At the beginning of May 1985, I was called to an appointment with the prison psychiatrist. He informed me that the Board of Prison Terms had approved my inclusion in the Cat T programme, as had been requested by a psychologist at Folsom almost a year earlier. I was to be transferred to the California Men's Colony, an institution where the programme was being established. Within a month I was on another bus, heading to another institution where I would have to start over. I hoped I could earn the credit to get me home in 12 more years. I still hadn't heard from Amy but hoped she would write to me – if for no other reason than to tell me how my son was.

16

California Men's Colony (CMC East)

California Men's Colony (CMC) is located near the city of
San Luis Obispo on the coast of central California, halfway
between Los Angeles and San Francisco. Due to the number of
celebrities who have served time there, it gained the nickname
"Home of the Stars". Arriving at CMC-East, a medium-security
facility, the first thing I noticed was the smell of a salty sea
breeze. This place was close to the Pacific Ocean.

After pulling into the institution, the bus made a circle
around a gun tower in the middle of a flower garden, before
finally stopping in a narrow drive between two buildings.
I stepped off the bus with around 10 other guys, three of
whom had come from Deuel Vocational Institution with
me. We were ushered through a side door and into a room
where two benches were bolted to the wall. This Receiving
and Release area felt quite relaxed – to start with, a very
effeminate guard asked one of the inmate clerks to see

if any of us needed a glass of water or something to eat. Rather than wait to hear our answer, the clerk just came out and gave us a boxed lunch and a half-pint carton of milk. He apologised there would be a delay before we were processed because the memo-graph machine was down, though someone was working on it. A couple of us were wondering if this was some kind of set-up.

About an hour later, a guard waved to one of the guys sitting on the other bench to come to the counter — what made the situation even more unbelievable was that he was smiling and joking with the new arrival. As soon as each guy went up, he was given a bedroll and told to take a seat on the benches. I realised they were calling us up in alphabetical order. Since I'd been listed as "Wetmore", I was last.

When it was my turn, the guard asked me if I had a problem with homosexuals, to which I responded that I didn't if they didn't have a problem with me. He laughed. After I'd answered his other questions and signed the form, one of the clerks came out to take us to our yards, which at California Men's Colony were called "quads". I was led to A Quad.

The clerk told me to walk through the turnstile. "When you get to the camera, look at it and clearly say your name," he said. "But don't push the posts too fast or the guard in the tower will stop them and you could bust your face." He then turned back the way we had come and took the others to another set of turnstiles about 100 feet away, marked B Quad.

A voice from a speaker inside the turnstile told me to get my ass in gear and move into the quad. Just as the clerk had explained, the guard in the tower suddenly stopped the turnstile; if I hadn't had my bedroll in front of me, I would have smashed my face. Once I was through, I reported to the quad office for cell assignment and the clerk ushered me to see the sergeant. Within just a couple of minutes, I knew he was a redneck from Bakersfield, mainly because of his accent.

The sergeant told me about all the opportunities at California Men's Colony. "I hope you'll take advantage of them," he said. "There are lots of notorious inmates here, many off death row with the classes of '72 and '76. At no time will aggression be accepted towards them or anyone else, whether staff or inmate. Here you should get all the tools you need to show the parole board you've been rehabilitated." He then shook my hand, wished me good luck and asked the clerk to show me to my building and cell.

As the clerk and I started walking around on the asphalt track encircling a grass yard, I was taken aback to see guys laying out on blankets getting suntans, as well as rubbing lotion on each other. As we got closer to Building 1, where my cell was, we had to walk on the grass to avoid four guys playing tennis doubles.

Stepping up on the porch of the building, I asked the clerk if this was normal here.

"Prepare yourself – you haven't seen the half of it yet," he replied, before walking me to the guard's station.

The guard at the podium was about five feet four inches tall and probably weighed 250 pounds, a far cry from the many guards I met at California Medical Facility, Folsom, San Quentin and Deuel Vocational Institution, who tended to be tall and physically fit. Here at California Men's Colony, I got the feeling it was more of a place for misfit guards and inmates. I wondered if somehow I'd been mis-classified. The guard handed me a key but I instinctively pulled away, as if he was handing me hot coals.

"Where did you just transfer in from?" he asked.

I told him. "DVI."

"Well, you'll find CMC nothing like DVI," he said as he handed over the key. "This is a key to your cell. You can come and go all you want between 6am and 10pm, except during the 4pm count."

My cell was number 1146. As my key had an "X" after the number, I'd be sleeping in the bunk that folded down off the wall. After unchaining my bunk and pulling it down, I put my bedroll on it and went to explore the yard and this new beautiful world I found myself in.

The yard was abuzz with activity, but everyone seemed to be doing what they wanted and no one seemed in charge. Guys of different races were working out, playing cards and tennis, or just walking around together – very different to the places I'd been previously. Walking over to an empty bench on the weight pile, I loaded up a bar with 175 pounds and thought I'd do a few reps. But no sooner had I started, than a red-haired guy came up to me.

"I'm Blaine, but I'm Native American so go by "Red Bear," he said. "Need a spotter?"

I politely declined his offer.

"Well I've been told by one of the clerks you're an Other. Thought you might like some information about the place."

I thought about it for a moment before answering. "Well I don't need help with such a small weight, but appreciate knowing anything you can tell me."

He told me about some of the more high-profile inmates here, including Charles "Tex" Watson and Bruce Davis, both part of the Manson family. I told him I'd met Charlie Manson at California Medical Facility but he wasn't that impressed.

"Tex runs the Protestant Chapel," Red Bear said. "Try not to run afoul of him, as many guards look out for him. Bruce Davis though is actually a decent fellow. They're both in A Quad, so you'll bump into them at some point. Richard and James Schoenfield are here too."

I looked at him blankly. "Their names don't ring a bell."

"Ah, well they're the Chowchilla Kidnappers. Took a bus of schoolchildren back in 1978." Pointing at the tennis courts, he added, "There they are, right there. They're always playing tennis."

Looking over, I saw two very tanned and athletic guys playing against people who seemed poorly matched to them. "I'm just here to do my time and don't want to be bothered by other people's issues," I said.

Red Bear then told me about the layout of California Men's Colony – explaining where to find the canteen, hobby shop, laundry room and Prison Industry Authority (PIA) shops, as well as vocational classes and the gym and where I could watch movies. Before getting up to leave, he told me he lived at the end of my tier and I should go to see him if I needed anything. About an hour later, a guy who looked like he could have been an NFL linebacker introduced himself as my new celly, Moose. Moose told me he was from Hemet in California and was serving 15 years to life, and suggested we go back to the cell and get it organised for the both of us.

The following morning after breakfast, the guard on my tier gave me a priority ducat, which stated I was to appear before the Yokefellows at the Protestant chapel at 10am, and that failure to do so would result in disciplinary action. This sort of threat had never applied to any priority ducat I had received in the past, even at the Level IV institutions. Since I didn't know who these Yokefellows were, I felt they were personally disrespecting me. I made sure when I went over there I was pumped, so if there was trouble I was ready.

Arriving at the chapel I was greeted by two guys collecting the ducats of the seven or eight of us who had received them.

They looked at us strangely, as if they were trying to size us up. Both of them were taller than me so I stared them straight in the eye with a blank expression. We were directed into the chapel and seated in the front pews. Looking around, I saw four more inmates, all wearing tags on their shirts that said "Inmate Deacon". Though none of these guys looked formidable, it looked as if they were on guard for something. After a few minutes, one of the guys announced that the pastor was going to be talking to us about our involvement in the Yokefellows programme. I stood up and asked why I'd been chosen, I had no interest in any organised religious programmes. He replied that it would be up to the pastor if I could leave or not. As I sat back down, my mood was beginning to darken.

Music started playing over the loudspeakers. Those of us in the pews looked back over our shoulders to see a tall figure walking up the aisle, with a spotlight shining behind him. When he reached the podium, he laid his bible down, opened it and introduced himself as "Pastor Watson". I realised this was "Tex" Watson of the Manson Family.

I stood up again, "I don't know what you're selling, but I'm not buying," I said. "Thanks very much for your invite, but I've no interest in you or your Yokefellows. So I'm out of here."

I walked towards the exit, but one of the Inmate Deacons blocked my way. Looking him straight in the face I asked him to move. He put his hand against my chest to prevent me from leaving.

"You believe in life after death?" I asked him in a low, calm voice. "Well if you don't take your hand off me, I'll give you the chance to find out."

He removed his hand and stepped aside, and I went back to the yard.

Almost a week later, I was told by the committee that I was being considered for the Cat T programme when it was introduced in the next couple of months. They said to look for my own job assignment – I had 30 days to do this. As I passed the medical department, I thought I'd apply there. At the reception desk, I spoke to a staff member, giving them a run down of my medical background and what I'd been doing at my last three institutions.

It turned out the man I spoke to was a medical technical assistant. He took my name and CDC number, and said he had to go talk to someone. While I was waiting, I looked around the room at the patients waiting for appointments and could tell that most of them were in pretty poor health – I figured I'd probably be hired rather quickly.

After around 20 minutes, the medical technical assistant returned, bringing two nurses.

"Oh, no, Mr Wetmore, you can't work in this hospital," one nurse said to me, and then the other one repeated it. "You have a crime of moral turpitude. We couldn't let you near any sick people. Why would you think we would want you?"

I wasn't just being told "no" but was being told "no" in stereo.

"So why have I been assigned medical jobs at the other prisons?" I asked them.

"The level of concern for patients must be lower at other places," they both replied. "There's no job for you here, Mr Wetmore."

As I returned to A Quad, struggling to believe that conversation, I heard someone call out, "Hey, Wetmore." I turned around to see a couple of the inmate deacons from the chapel.

"Pastor Watson wants to talk to you," they said. "He's willing to forgive your childish behaviour. You'll find him on a set of bleachers, finishing his sermon for Sunday. Follow us."

I figured this was going to be interesting, so I let them lead the way. As I arrived at the bleacher "Tex" looked up and invited me to sit on the bench at his feet. But instead, I sat next to him on the top bench.

He started to speak to me by calling me "Sinner Wetmore", at which point I put up my hand.

"It's not Wetmore, it's Kane – and not like the biblical Cain, but K-A-N-E," I said.

He stared at me for a minute. "Apparently you didn't realise I had personally issued that ducat to you and was offering you a great opportunity to become one of my Yokefellow Disciples."

It was almost like hearing Dr Wetmore talking to me. So I decided to stop the conversation.

"I don't believe in Christianity. And if I did want to study the Bible, you'd be the last person I'd seek out to learn about Jesus."

"Don't you want to go to heaven?" he asked.

"No thank you – I'd rather go to Tir na nOg," I said, as I turned around and smiled at him. Then I walked off the bleachers, leaving him to figure out that Tir na nOg is the afterlife for Celts.

This was my first run-in with Charles "Tex" Watson, Charlie Manson's right-hand man. He was seen as charming, attractive and athletic back then, and it was apparently his charm that attracted girls to the ranch to join the Manson family. He seemed to use this ability in much the same way in prison, getting guards to allow him to do things inmates weren't supposed to do, such as issuing ducats and persuading inmates to follow his "Gospel According to Tex" teachings.

After our interaction, I was hoping there wouldn't be any more. But just a few days later, while sitting down to dinner, one of the guys at my table turned out to be Bruce Davis, another member of the Family. The murders he was in prison for weren't the ones Manson was best known for, but it would always be his connection to Charlie and Tex Watson that would stop him from being paroled.

Davis had earned a PhD in Philosophy while in prison, and I found his conversation far more interesting than that of the average inmate. Because of his intelligence and quiet manners, I would find myself having many discussions with him over the years. He mentioned that he'd heard I'd not got on well with Tex. So I asked him how well he got on with him.

"Render unto Caesar that which is Caesar's and to God that which is God's," he replied. "And I'm long through with Caesar."

I took this to mean he'd fallen out with Charlie Manson and Charles Watson. Having known Bruce the entire time I was at California Men's Colony, I can say he was one of the most humble and kind men I met in prison and unrecognisable from the man he'd been when he committed his crimes. I saw him at least a couple of times a week, and we'd often challenge each other on a variety of subjects, which was both enjoyable and mentally stimulating.

Strangely enough Tex founded an outreach organisation, Abounding Love Ministries, while at California Men's Colony. He wrote books titled *Will You Die For Me?*, *Manson's Right-Hand Man*, *Illumination Bible Charts*, *Our Identity, Spirit, Soul and Body* and *Christian Fools*, and would charge inmates $20 if they wanted a book signed. Since all proceeds from his books went to his ministry, which was managed by his wife, she was able to claim state welfare benefits for her children.

Within two weeks of having been turned down for a job in the medical department, I'd successfully applied for a job at the prison shoe factory learning how to lay soles on shoes and boots for jails, prisons and other state institutions. We even shipped about 3,000 pairs to the Guatemalan army. I worked there for three and a half years, doing everything from sole-laying to quality control and making the cardboard boxes in which the shoes were shipped. I went from a labourer to an assistant lead man in no time.

By the autumn of my first year at California Men's Colony, I only hung around with two people: Red Bear and a Romanian guy named Tibor, though we called him Ted, who became my dependable weight training partner. Even though Ted could match me pound for pound on the bars, he was able to get great definition, when all I did was bulk up. Red Bear would sit at the weights and offer encouragement to both of us while eating candy bars, ice cream and sodas – 12 ounces was the limit to his weight lifting.

Then just before Christmas, while walking laps with Ted after a workout I saw a guy named Jim. I could tell he'd been a thalidomide baby and though he was about five foot eight, he only weighed about 100 pounds. Ted told me that Jim had been a professional pool hustler on the streets. He'd apparently won a $100,000 bet on a series of games, but the other guy refused to pay up and pushed Jim to the ground, at which point Jim beat the guy to death with a pool cue and collected his money. Jim was arrested while drunk, passed out in his car in the parking lot of the pool hall, about an hour later. The District Attorney called it robbery and murder, and Jim was sentenced to life without parole. Because of his physical disability, he had a stunted arm, he was often the victim of abuse by other inmates. Here at California Men's Colony, people would take things from him. Because he was afraid of going somewhere more violent, he tolerated it in silence.

Jim was coming through the turnstile struggling with a box. As he started walking across the grass to his cell on the second tier of Building 1, I noticed two of Tex's deacons from the chapel start to shadow him. I knew what was about to happen and headed towards them. Ted was telling me not to get involved. I told him he didn't need to come along but I had to make sure Jim got home with his package safely. In that moment, the two churchmen had pushed Jim over and were walking away with his box and I could hear them laughing. As I reached within striking distance, I glanced at the tower to see if the gunner was looking before I struck.

I hit the guy carrying the box right at the base of his skull. His legs folded like a marionette whose strings had been cut. I reached down, tossed the box to Ted and turned to face the other guy.

"Hey, why did you do that?" he said.

"You bible-thumping guys just robbed someone who can't defend himself," I replied.

To my surprise, he said that it wasn't robbery, but that "Flipper" (referring to Jim) had to pay rent to stay on the yard.

"Wait a minute," I said. "You haven't tried to charge me rent, so what gives you the right to charge him?"

"Well look at the freak – he's like that because his mother had sex with Satan," said the other guy who was now getting up from the ground.

I realised that he believed it. In one quick movement I peeled off my shirt and proudly displayed my left bicep, which bore a tattoo of my motorcycle club patch.

"I'm a Confederate Devil and he doesn't pay any more rent," I said. "If anyone has a problem, tell them to come see me – and that includes your boss Tex."

The two guys were stunned. As they scurried away, Ted and I gave Jim back his box. We turned down his offer to give us something from it, before continuing our laps as if nothing had happened.

Later that day Jim showed up with an armful of food, wanting to pay me. I explained I appreciated the offer but didn't need anything. But he said if I ever needed anything I should ask him and he would get it. I wondered if those two guys were going to report me. I'd so badly wanted to just do my time and not try to "fix" things – after all, that's what had got me into prison in the first place.

Tex Watson's manipulative and domineering treatment of inmates who wished to participate in programmes and services in the Protestant chapel was by now a daily occurence. The prison officials had turned a blind eye to complaints by other inmates about what Tex was doing in the chapel. But in March 1987, he was finally removed from his position of prison inmate chaplain. The prison discovered that he had bullied inmates and prevented those who objected to how he ran the chapel from attending services and programmes. Even this didn't get him to clean up his act and I would have to confront him on a number of further occasions over the years.

In about 1988, I became aware of a guy on A Quad named Herbert Mullin, though everyone called him "Herbie". To me, he was just another of the characters at California Men's Colony. He would often be found dancing in the middle of the yard at night, staring up at the stars. Once, he saw me coming back from the hobby shop at about 9:30pm and asked me to listen to his headphones. Being polite, I put them on and waited. After a couple of minutes passed with no sound, I took off the headphones and noticed that the end of the cord was in his hand.

"What was I supposed to hear?" I asked him.

"The universe, man – the sounds of the universe," he replied with a grin.

I thanked him and returned to my cell. It was only when I asked about him the next day that I discovered who he was.

Herbert Mullin was referred to as "the Earthquake Killer". He had, between October 1972 and February 1973, committed 10 murders because voices in his head had told him that killing these people would prevent a massive earthquake in California. His victims were a homeless man, a priest, a girl hitch-hiker, four boys in a forest, a friend, the friend's wife and the woman who told him to find his friend. He admitted to the murders but said in court it couldn't be proven that he didn't prevent the earthquakes from happening. He wasn't spared the death penalty because he may have been suffering from a mental defect during his crimes. Instead he was sentenced to 10 life sentences. When I knew him between 1986 and 1992, I found him to be a pleasant individual who, if he had received help early in his life, would in all likelihood never have committed these crimes. He's currently incarcerated in Mule Creek State Prison.

Larry Singleton was another inmate. He was housed in B Quad in CMC East, where the most serious sex offenders were kept. In 1978, he picked up a 15-year-old hitch-hiker called Mary Vincent. He raped her and cut off both her forearms with a hatchet, before throwing her off a 30-foot cliff outside Modesto, leaving her naked and almost dead. She managed to climb back up the cliff and a passer-by took her to hospital. Larry was sentenced to 14 years in prison, the maximum allowed for mayhem and rape in California at that time. He worked as a teaching assistant in prison, which reduced his sentence, and he only served eight of the 14 years.

In 1987, the outcry from the public over his release led to the Singleton Bill, which changed the sentence for his crime to 25 years to life. Because of public rage about the cases of Larry Singleton and the kidnapper and murderer Archie Fain, in 1989 the California legislation took away the half-time work and good behaviour credits for lifers and allowed the state governor to reverse parole board decisions. This sent shockwaves through the California prison system regarding the sentences of life-term inmates who'd been in prison before these two legislative decisions were made – they'd effectively changed the laws we'd been sentenced under and increased the amount of time we would serve. So I would now have to wait until 1999 to go before a parole board, and the state governor could take away any parole grant I was given if he chose to do so.

In early 1988, I was called to my counsellor's office and was told that my son, Mark, had passed away after being knocked down by a drunk driver. I couldn't accept the news – my son had been the sole focus for me trying to get home. Instead of receiving a letter with comforting words from Amy, I had an impersonal statement from the prison counsellor who then dismissed me without no thought about how this news might affect me. It was a pain I would have to bear alone.

You might think it couldn't get worse, but it did when the same counsellor called me to his office only a few months later to inform me that Amy was seeking child support for our other two children. It turned out she'd had a daughter and a son with a guy she'd hooked up with after getting out of prison. But he didn't want to be their father. Since technically she was still married to me, she'd put me down as their father on the birth records. Realising my counsellor wasn't the sharpest, I tried to explain to him that I couldn't possibly be the father of these children. I hadn't seen my wife since I'd left Fresno County Jail, years before their births.

He then said the stupidest thing I ever heard. "Mothers always know who their children's fathers are."

Since I was making only pennies an hour, they couldn't really take any money from me, so the child support unit in Fresno County asked to be notified when I was released and said they would pursue the matter then.

After years of fighting over correcting my name from John Raymond Wetmore to Morgan James Kane, I finally received some of the best news I'd had in prison. An official document arrived, stating that from 30 October 1990 I was to be known as Morgan James Kane. I chose to go by Jamie for ease. But when I took it to my counsellor he said he didn't care. I would have to continue this fight for many years to come.

Soon, I was offered the opportunity to move over to working in the prison laundry. This might not sound like a good opportunity, but I was able to work the first watch shift, which ran from 10pm until 6am. I would also be paid

60 cents an hour instead of the 45 cents I'd been making in the shoe factory. As part of the job I would be allowed to drive the "Goat", a small tractor used to manoeuvre planes at airports that we used to take empty dirty clothes carts to the quads and bring back the full ones. Because the Goat was kept outside the security fence, it was generally brought into the facility by one of the garage workers. But when heavy fog would roll in, I was given the responsibility to collect it, leaving the perimeter of CMC East with only the tower gunner to prevent me from escaping. It may seem strange, but at no time while I was outside the perimeter fence did I entertain the thought of escaping – I knew that to do so would jeopardise my opportunity to go home, even though I now had no son waiting for me.

I found it easy to get accustomed to life at California Men's Colony, as there were so many programmes to participate in. Inmate bands played on the quads every weekend and physical altercations were rare. Everyone acted as if the life they were living was all there was in the world. With the changes in the law regarding lifers, it didn't seem that any of us would go home, a feeling reinforced by the election of Pete Wilson as California state governor, who declared a "No parole for any lifer" policy.

I was comfortable going to work, working out on the weight pile and doing my hobbies without having to constantly look over my shoulder. One thing I didn't enjoy though was that all lifers had to do psych therapy classes. I'd come to California Men's Colony for the Cat T programme but it took almost two years for them to set this up, by which time there were about 200 guys waiting for it. They were only allowing 20 inmates on it at a time and the programme was to last 18 months. We were all re-interviewed. It was determined that I didn't need the programme, as I was managing my post-traumatic stress disorder (PTSD) well. But was I? Or was it just that I'd learned to suppress my nightmares and mistrust of others?

17

In the summer of 1990, my cellmate Moose was given a transfer down to California Institution for Men, near Chino. It was a hardship transfer, which was something you could apply for but was rarely granted. In his case, his mother was elderly and in a wheelchair from polio. Moose had support from organisations that applied pressure on prison officials to make the transfer happen. I was really pleased for him but I was also sad as he was the best celly I ever had. With Ted having transferred months earlier and Red Bear living with another native, I didn't have many options.

The day after Moose left, Jim asked if I'd like to move in with him — his celly was being paroled in a couple of days, and there was no one else he could trust. I figured it might be a good move, since I worked nights and would be gone almost every day a week and he went out to play chess and cards for money during the day, since he didn't have a job. The guards liked the fact that they could then use my cell on the first tier for someone with mobility problems, so the move happened three days later.

Around this time, a guy called Richard Alan Davis moved on to the second tier of my cell block, where he stayed from 1990 until 1993. He was spiteful and malicious to everyone, especially his celly, who he would make stay out of the cell when he was in it. He is most well known for the killing of Polly Klaas, and was the primary catalyst for California's "Three Strike Law". From an early age, he had a history of torturing and killing animals, and between 1967 and 1985 he had committed more than 25 serious felonies. After he was paroled in June 1993, he went on to kidnap, sexually assault and murder Polly in October of the same year. He was sentenced to death in August 1996 and is still on death row in San Quentin.

Jim was an intelligent person and we would have long discussions. I told him about motorcycles and the bike runs I'd been on, and he would tell me stories about travelling the world, playing pool for people who backed him in games where the stakes were up to half a million dollars for a series. But he didn't tell me about the particulars of his case and he never asked about mine. One thing I didn't know when I moved in with him was that our cell was directly below Tex Watson's.

Not too long after Jim and I had become cellies, I was coming out of A Quad one day to go to the library. I'd just gone through the turnstile and, to my surprise, who should I see but Wesley Tucker, the Aryan Brotherhood guy who had given me grief at Folsom. He'd just come out of the Education Office door. When he saw me, he gave a squeal and ran as fast as he could to the B Quad. I was amused, as I knew the only way a documented gang member could get to California Men's Colony was to tell on the others of their gang. Wesley must have fallen from grace with the Aryan Brotherhood and they would have placed a "kill on sight" order on him, leaving him looking over his shoulder forever.

While sitting in the library, I looked up from my book to find members of the Goon Squad, who told me to come with them. I was escorted to their office, where their sergeant and lieutenant were waiting for me. After being roughly seated in a chair, I was interrogated about my intentions towards Wesley Tucker. I calmly assured them that I didn't care about him at all and just wanted to do my programme.

We know you had problems with him at Folsom," they said. "You still holding a grudge?"

"If you read the reports you'll see he had a problem with me, I didn't want to be a part of his prison gang."

"Wesley is now a protective witness for the federal authorities," said the lieutenant. "He'll be testifying against the Aryan Brotherhood and the Aryan Nation Church."

"As I said, I've no interest in him or any of the problems he's brought on himself."

Then they brought Wesley in from another room. He'd

been listening to what I'd said.

Satisfied I meant him no harm, he stuck out his hand. "No hard feelings then?"

Pausing only a moment, I shook his hand and was free to go about my business.

A few weeks later, two more Aryan Brotherhood guys arrived at California Men's Colony and were put on B Quad for their protection. Then the day before Wesley was to be taken to the federal court house to testify, he was found stabbed to death in his cell. It turned out that the two Aryan Brotherhood guys had been given the permission to tell on other gang members, just so they could get to him. But once they'd been debriefed, they would also now have targets on their backs for the rest of their lives, which is how gang life in Californian prisons works.

One day in November 1991, the prison chapels (Protestant, Catholic and Jewish), put out notices that inmates could get two cards for Christmas or Chanukah from each chapel, without having to attend services. I collected cards from both the Catholic and Jewish chapels first. When I arrived at the Protestant chapel, I saw three inmate deacons trying to nail a stand into the bottom of an 8-foot spruce tree, splintering the trunk with every nail they struck in. On seeing me, they asked what I wanted, so I told them I'd come for my two Christmas cards. Tex came out of the pastor's office to tell me I had to attend services if I wanted them.

"This wasn't what the notice said," I told Tex.

"The Protestant chaplain has changed it."

I could see the chaplain through the window and said I'd like to speak to him myself, but Tex refused.

"If you don't leave, I'll have to ask the chaplain to call guards to remove you," he said.

I turned to go.

"Why do you want Christmas cards," asked one of the deacons. "You don't even believe in Jesus. You're a pagan."

I spun around. "Don't you know Jesus wasn't actually born in mid-winter?" I said to him. "All the symbols at this time of year come from pagans – the yule log, holly and ivy, hanging of mistletoe… and especially that "solstice" tree you're showing so much disrespect for."

I decided to file a grievance against the chaplain. I knew it was the only way I could get him to talk to me. If he didn't want the complaint to go into his personnel file he had to make the effort to resolve the problem. Sure enough, he called me to the chapel about a week later. When I'd made my complaint I mentioned the disdain I'd received from his inmate pastor and deacons over not being a Christian and wanting non-Christian cards. At first, the chaplain said he didn't think he had any non-Christian cards available.

"Well I can prove your staff has been selling them," I replied.

He remembered he might have some in his desk drawer,

and pulled out a box. I could tell by the size and envelopes these were non-religious Hallmark ones. I found one with the picture of a stag running through a forest and another of a nativity scene with Mary, Joseph and the Three Wise Men around baby Jesus while Santa Claus handed him a candy cane. The chaplain didn't understand this choice, until I explained that Santa Claus wasn't a Christian either. I thanked him and left, rather happy with myself.

A few days later, Jim came back to our cell, having tried to get cards only to be told they were all out. Yet he'd watched more than a dozen people get them from the Protestant chapel. He was fed up with people treating him like he was nothing and was making a knife when I walked in. It was his full intention to stab Tex Watson.

"This will definitely raise your profile," I said. "You'll probably start getting Christmas cards from the Sharon Tate crime victims groups."

We both laughed. I calmed him down and told him to let me handle it.

On Christmas Eve, I borrowed the tape of *The White Album* by The Beatles from another inmate. We'd been told we would all be locked in our cells from 11pm until 6am so the guards could have a Christmas party. I waited patiently. At the stroke of midnight, I started playing 'Helter Skelter' through the vent system up to Tex's cell, and only stopped at about 5am, at which time I slid the tape out of the cell and across to another cell.

Just as expected, when the cells were unlocked at 6am a couple of guards asked me about the incident Tex had reported. Jim and I both told them we knew nothing about it, and Jim added that maybe Tex was having a flashback. While we were at breakfast, our cell was searched for the tape, which had already been transported back to its owner. When I saw Tex later that day, I asked him if he slept well.

As mentioned earlier, California Men's Colony was known as the "Home of the Stars". In 1991, we had Ike Turner as an inmate. Though he was primarily housed at the West facility, he stayed in our hospital ward in the East and would often sit outside and entertain inmates who wanted to wish him well. Additionally Christian Brando, the son of actor Marlon Brando who had been convicted of manslaughter, arrived in 1991. When he arrived at CMC East, he was housed in D Quad facility, where most of mental health inmates were housed, as it was believed he would be least likely to be recognised there.

He was given the job of working on the back dock of the kitchen, right in front of the guard's workstation so they could keep an eye on him. At that time I was working in the prison laundry. One of my duties was to deliver cleaning rags to the kitchen, so I had near-daily interactions with Christian. He was a bit stand-offish as a number of inmates had tried to get him to give them money, drugs or help with their legal cases, and he was constantly being asked for his autograph by staff and inmates. His father was allowed to visit him on non-visiting days and was often also subjected to autograph request by members of staff.

We were allowed to take photos on the quads. As with most other institutions, we had inmate photographers with Polaroid cameras who charged $1 yard ducat per photo. There was also a programme where guys would volunteer to go over to D Quad at weekends to try to get some of the more heavily medicated guys out to the yard and to interact with other inmates. These volunteers wore orange baseball caps to help designate them to staff. It just so happened that in the summer of 1992, a guy I worked with in the laundry was one of these volunteers. When he learnt that Christian was on D Quad, he hatched a plan to make a little money.

This guy had heard about the *National Enquirer* and figured that if he got a photo, the publication would run it and he might make $500. His plan was simple: he would go to D Quad as usual, where he knew Christian liked to watch the softball game, and he arranged for the yard photographer to take a picture of him and Christian together. He walked up behind Christian and positioned himself so when he tapped Christian on the shoulder, it would look like they were about to kiss. He sent the photo with the title 'Christian Brando is my Prison Love Slave' and sent it to the *National Enquirer*, thinking they would send him some money.

He'd been waiting about two weeks, thinking he'd shortly

have about $500 – what he'd heard the *National Enquirer* paid for such stories. At about 2am one morning while we were working in the laundry, we heard a rumble of heavy footsteps coming down the walkway. The doors burst open and standing there were all 12 members of the Goon Squad and their sergeant and lieutenant – some of the biggest guards we'd ever seen. The lieutenant called out the name of the inmate who'd had the picture taken. A moment before, he'd been standing next to me by the washing machine but now he was nowhere to be seen. Just before the Goon Squad could look for him, an inmate standing next to an industrial dryer signalled to the officers that the person they were looking for was hiding inside it.

We all watched the sergeant walk over to the dryer, accompanied by two of the guards. Seeing the door was ajar, he closed and locked it and turned the dryer on. Even though it was filled with clothes, a couple of seconds later we heard loud banging and screaming from inside. The sergeant allowed this to continue for nearly a minute before turning the dryer off. Once the spinning had stopped, the guards opened the door, pulled the inmate out and threw him to the floor, before cuffing and leg chaining him. Then the officers dragged him out of the laundry, his face bouncing off the ground. We could hear his screams all the way back to their office.

Later on, I was standing on the loading dock preparing a truck when we watched two cars and a van leaving the institution and I realised he'd been transferred out. The following day I saw on the movement sheet that he'd been sent to Tehachapi, one of the worst Ad Seg units outside of Folsom or San Quentin.

On 1 April, I was called away from the laundry at about 8.30am, during an overtime shift, to appear before a classification committee. Without warning, they informed me that as new CDC regulations stated that Level II lifers were to be removed from Level III institutions to make room for those with higher points, I was to be moved. They gave me two options: Tehachapi or Folsom.

I questioned them about Folsom because, as far as I knew, it was a Level IV institution only. The captain replied that while on paper it was still technically only a Level IV, CDC had determined to change the population so it would primarily be a Level II facility and they would be shipping all the Level IV inmates out. Having been to Folsom, I knew this forced conversion would bring about a lot of bloodshed. I didn't want to be a part of it, so I chose Tehachapi.

Over the next couple of weeks, more than 600 lifers were determined to have Level II points and were notified that they would be getting shipped out soon. This was devastating, as many of them had been at California Men's Colony for as long as 25 years and feared they would be sent to a yard where stabbings would be a daily event. In fact, between the time I went to the committee and the first week of May when I was shipped out, there had been more than 50 attempted suicides and more than a dozen successful ones. Some men were so desperate to stay at California Men's Colony that they injected themselves with the HIV-contaminated blood of inmates who were positive, as those with HIV couldn't be transferred. This really showed how paralysing fear could be – and yet I always found fear a challenge that I wanted to face and conquer.

Imagine my surprise when I climbed on the bus taking me to Tehachapi and found Tex Watson sitting right behind me. When I looked around, I saw Herbie Mullins sitting a few seats away. I knew both of them were going to Mule Creek State Prison – because of their notoriety they would need protection at most general population facilities.

I was sitting on the right hand side of the bus so I could watch inmate property being loaded on. I recognised mine among a stack of boxes; looking at the destination label where it had said Tehachapi, the name was crossed out and with a black marker pen, someone had written "FOLSOM". All I could think, as the bus pulled out of California Men's Colony, was "Ding, ding, here comes round two."

18

Wasco State Prison

The ride back to Folsom was a long one, which was fine by me as I had a lot of thinking to do. I knew there would be fragments of the Aryan Brotherhood still there who would certainly know of me, and they were hardly likely to forgive and forget. I figured I was going backwards in time and wondered if this would be my undoing, as I would have to be on high alert from the moment I stepped off the bus and had no allies I could trust.

Having been at California Men's Colony for nearly seven years with its laid-back attitude and no-nonsense allowance for violence, I was now returning to a place of madness and despair, where violence was daily. Would my skills be sharp enough? I was almost 10 years older. Would my reaction time have slowed down too much? I had surgery just a couple of years back to replace a bone in my hand, from when I broke it on Pineapple's face, and it still caused me a bit of pain, particularly when it was cold.

The worst thing about this trip so far was that Tex Watson suddenly wanted to be my friend. He tried talking to me all the way – a big problem as the guards on the bus had made it very clear we were only allowed to speak in a low voice to the person sitting beside us. They'd only placed one inmate on each seat so there was actually nobody sitting beside anyone else. I'm sure in some sick mind they thought this was funny and it gave them a reason to yell at us. Tex was extremely nervous and concerned about this transfer because he'd been at California Men's Colony since he'd come off death row in 1972. He knew there were rumours that a bounty would be paid to anyone who killed him by family members of La Bianca.

I'd hoped for a quick and straight-through ride that would get me to Folsom. But nothing was straightforward in my life, it would seem. So instead of heading straight north, the bus went north-west and we ended up pulling into California Training Facility near Soledad. Not only were we dropping off inmates and picking others up, but this was where we would spend the night. As we came into the Receiving and Release unit and were ushered into a holding tank, a fight suddenly started between two Hispanic inmates and a guard at the counter, which resulted in all of us getting pepper-sprayed as other guards responded to the alarm. So now we were crammed together, 30 guys in a cell made for 12, properly seasoned and sweating from the heat. I just knew this was going to be a bad trip.

We had arrived at 1pm, but it took until 3am to place us in overnight accommodation cells where we could get some sleep. Wouldn't you know it though – at 4.30am, we were woken up and given peanut butter sandwiches for breakfast before being taken back, shackled and put back on the bus to continue our trip. Of course I ended up with Tex sitting right behind me again. His attempt at conversation got us yelled at by the guards a number of times before we reached our next destination of California Men's Colony at Vacaville.

Luckily, this was only a short stopover, before we continued on to CMF South, a new facility that had been built only a few years earlier, again exchanging inmates before finally getting back on the road. Now we were heading to Mule Creek State Prison, where they would be dropping off all but two of us. The closer we were to the next stop, the quieter the bus became; those staying there were starting to take in that they were going to a place specifically designated for protective custody.

At Mule Creek, the guards came on the bus to take inmates off, but took all of them except for Tex Watson and the two of us going to Folsom.

"What do you think's going to happen to us?" Tex asked me.

"Well, me and the guy over there are going to Folsom but I think you're screwed," I replied.

He sat back in his seat and I heard what sounded like soft sobbing. Suddenly there was tapping at the window where we were sitting and I saw a guard unloading inmate property from the cargo hold beneath us. He held up a box with Tex's name on it, one that was marked "Fragile" and "This side up". While smiling at Tex, he turned the box upside down and slammed it down to the ground. He then kicked it around 10 feet to the building.

"That's my word processor," Tex hollered. "The court allows me to have it. Please be careful."

In response, the guard continued to unload, throwing each box at, or on top of, the word processor box. When he was finished, he went back inside.

A few minutes later, the sergeant boarded the bus. He looked the three of us over, with a big grin on his face.

"Will Mr Charles Tex Watson come on down?" he said in game-show style. "You're the next contestant on The Price is Right."

Tex stood up slowly and moved to the front of the bus. The sergeant ushered him off and took him to the outside wall of the Receiving and Release unit. Six guards were standing there. Immediately, they put Tex's face against the wall and all began screaming at him incoherently. This went on for close to five minutes before they finally dragged him inside the building.

The other guy and I, still on the bus, spoke almost together, "Sure glad that's not me."

Around fifteen minutes later, the sergeant reappeared and said that there was a change in our destination.

Please don't tell me I'm staying here at Mule Creek, I thought, as I just knew if that happened I'd end up as Tex's celly.

After giving us a moment to take in what he'd just said, the sergeant finally decided to enlighten us. "You're being rerouted to Wasco State Prison."

The other guy spoke up first. "Why is that, and where the hell is Wasco?"

The sergeant explained that due to stabbings of Level IIs at Folsom, by the Level IV inmates, a directive from the Department of Corrections in Sacramento had ordered that all Level II transfers to Folsom were redirected.

"Wasco State Prison is in Kern County down near Bakersfield."

" Is Wasco a Level II institution?" I asked.

"To my knowledge, it's a Reception Centre, taken over from California Medical Facility for Northern California," the sergeant replied. He tossed each of us a paper bag containing a peanut butter sandwich and an apple, and left us.

Even though neither one of us spoke it out loud, I reckon we both thought we were the ones who were screwed. We were back on the road now heading towards Wasco State Prison.

It must have been the middle of the night when we arrived at our new destination. By now the bus team had been active for almost 24 hours, so they were surly and nasty and physically dragged us off the steps of the bus into the

Wasco Receiving and Release unit. It didn't help when the receiving officer said he had no paperwork for us. At least this provided us with a little entertainment, as the tired bus sergeant grabbed the shirt of the receiving guard and told him he was accepting us or else he was going to get his ass kicked. The receiving officer placed us all in a holding tank and informed us we wouldn't be processed to enter the institution until official transfer papers had arrived from Sacramento.

At almost 8am, we were woken up by a guard shouting, "Come and get your chow." As we reached the bars, we were each handed a paper tray with three pancakes and syrup, a bit of porridge that had been spilled mostly on the pancakes and a carton of milk. The breakfast was cold and, for the most part, flavourless. The experience was enhanced by a couple of guys having to do bowel movements in the open toilet in our tank. It would be a few hours before we would be moved to Yard A in the mainline facility.

As we left the Receiving and Release unit one of the inmates asked the two escorting officers when we would get our property.

"Within a few days," was the short reply.

We proceeded to Yard A. Surprisingly, lined up on the opposite side of the walkway were about 50 reception inmates. It wasn't normal procedure to allow mainline and reception inmates to interact, with the exception of clerks. Just as we were moving with the middle section, three reception inmates started to stab one another. Almost immediately a tower gunner fired three or four shots, hitting one of the attackers and the guy being stabbed. One of the rounds had ricocheted off the concrete walkway and struck one of the guys from my bus. The bullet hit him in the lower abdomen. He was only two guys away from me, so I realised how close it was.

Lying face down on the walkway, I wondered if the gunner was going to fire again. But then I heard radio chatter and could hear running footsteps all around. Taking a chance to glance up slightly, I saw all the guards had handheld radios. They were also carrying PR-24 side handle batons. The PR-24 was the one issued to the Navy Shore Patrol and Marine Brig staff. When I'd been assigned to do medical for the prisoners in the brig at 32 St Naval Station, I'd been trained to use one. I realised no one could ever know this or I could be seen as a security risk.

It took around 10 minutes to get three rolling gurneys to the scene and pick up the wounded, I hoped the medical staff here were competent and had already made the call for an outside ambulance or two. I knew these injuries weren't just scratches or flesh wounds – without proper care, at least one of these guys might die.

Once on the yard, we were led to the sets of buildings. As we crossed the grass I noticed about a half a dozen guys or so milling around watching our little troupe arrive. I had a strange feeling about this, as this yard was bigger than about two-thirds of the whole institution of California Men's Colony, yet there was nobody here. I thought maybe they were all at job assignments.

As usual the procedure was to drop one or two of us off at each building. From behind the guard's desk, a short rather dumpy female officer with buck teeth gave me a list of empty cell numbers. She told me to go and look at them and let her know where I wanted to live. Walking away, I felt as though I'd been talking to a used car salesman and was being sold a lemon, because everywhere else we were always told which cell to go to.

The inmate who was cleaning nearby explained to me that there were currently only about 25 inmates in each building, though at capacity these could hold 200. This yard had only recently been activated.

"How much time you brought?" he asked me.

"I'm a lifer."

"The warden isn't going to like that." He explained that the warden had gone on local TV and said he would never allow life-term inmates on his mainline, but apparently CDC Headquarters in Sacramento had over-ridden him. I could see this wouldn't be a good thing.

Each institution went by a procedure manual called the Departmental Operations Manual, but they were also allowed to add additional rules. Here at Wasco, the warden had made the decision that lifers couldn't work in job assignments off the yard, which meant no Prison Industry Authority jobs, no plant ops jobs and, most importantly no vocational training. The parole boards demanded all lifers had at least two types of vocational training before they could even possibly be considered for release. In Wasco, the only jobs that lifers were going to be allowed were cleaning up the yard, cleaning up in their building or, in my case, getting one of the few jobs working in the education class as a teacher's aide.

Every week, there would be another 20 or so guys added to the yard. Two weeks after my arrival, we got word the guy who'd arrived with us, who had "accidentally" been shot, had died. He was serving only a three-year sentence for stealing a car and had less than six months to go. About a month after hearing that news, I saw Iron Mike and another guy Juan show up, two of the guys who had been in the 300lb Club at Deuel Vocational Institution. Juan regularly worked out with more than 600lbs on the bench, and somehow he and Mike got jobs monitoring the weight pile, which included stacking them up every night. So the two most muscular guys on the yard got to lift weights all day, which made them happy.

The yard was finally full by the time I'd been there for six months, and there was a weird vibe of mounting tension. There were no defined shot callers, but there were a lot of small groups. Elsewhere they would be united. One of these small groups was the Fresno Bulldogs. Here, they were the most organised so tended to be the ones in charge of the drugs coming in to the institution. On Yard A, drug debts were the main cause of stabbings, with gambling being the second cause. As I didn't do either, I was just an observer.

At my classification here, it had been decided I was "too white" to be an Other. So I was now listed as White, which caused problems as Whites thought I was a homeboy and somehow had to share with them, or help them get things. This meant when one of them got into a gambling or drug debt, they expected me to help, either by chipping in to pay it or by being willing to fight. They couldn't seem to wrap their minds around my unwillingness to do either. I did have to throw a few punches to get this point across, but none of these fights were that serious, as they were 20 year olds sucked up by drug use – trying to figure out how to do their time and survive life. Most were petty thieves on the outside stealing for their habits.

Finally, after I had been there a year, I had been given the assignment as a GED [General Educational Development] clerk, helping inmates earn their High School equivalence diploma. I chose to make waves with the prison administration, hoping they would ship me out of this brain drain place. So I filed an appeal, stating they were intentionally preventing lifers from being able to meet the parole board requirements for release by denying us vocational classes. I knew this would upset them. Rather than alter their rules, allowing us to leave the yard and go to the classes, they would have to ship me to keep this from going any further.

Less than two weeks later, a cart with a Brother 2050 word processor, an electric typewriter and a 10-key calculator rolled in – with the books and supplies to enable inmates to earn a certificate on the office devices course. Of course I had to take the course since I'd argued for a vocation. The teacher would come around every couple of weeks to see if anyone was ready for testing.

Some guys were unhappy as they were glad to have an excuse for the board, but a few were amazed and surprised that it happened and also how quickly. For me, this was one more thing holding me up from getting out of here, so I knuckled down and took the course. The diploma for completion of the course would be the first official document issued to me as Morgan James Kane, though the rest of my file still listed me as "Wetmore", including my ID card.

Since that first shooting, when I arrived here at Wasco, there had been none on our yard. Though the reception side was averaging at least one a month and, interestingly enough, the gunners would shoot the leg of the suspected attacker to stop him. Even though this didn't kill the inmate, the medical protocol at Wasco was that the leg would be removed. It was thought easier to heal the wound that way, with the least chance for infection, rather than trying to heal a bullet wound from the inside out. So the number of one-legged guys coming out of prison was rising. The other big health problem we had was valley fever, which was particularly serious for Blacks, Filipinos and those with weakened immune systems. During the last summer alone, more than 200 inmates became sick from it, and it was reported that three had died.

It was now almost Thanksgiving of 1994. Things had been reasonably calm, with our last lock-down having ended more than a month ago. Most guys tend to act right over the holidays, as that's when they were most likely to get visits from their families.

The day before Thanksgiving, a news expose programme on TV spoke about CDC having a large amount of sex offenders but not having the facilities to offer protection to all those requesting it from them. CDC had come up with a plan to quietly place a few sex offenders at a time on newly opening institution's yards, hoping they would go undiscovered, as there were quite a few institutions being built. The news showed pictures of the sex offenders and recited their crimes in pretty graphic details and then stated where they were currently housed.

Over 50 sex offenders had been placed at Wasco. Within minutes of the information being broadcasted, alarms were going off, not only in my building but all across Yard A. Cellies of these guys were beating them up and, in a few cases, stabbing them. We were now on lock down, as CDC tried to figure out how they would cover up this mess. At most places, inmates demanded to see each other's "paperwork", so they could check on their charges. Another problem was that within certain gangs found out that some of their muscle and even shot callers, were rapists and paedophiles.

As part of the fallout, during the first week of January 1995 a number of us older lifers were offered the opportunity to get transferred. We all took it. The choices were California Institution for Men (CIM) or Tehachapi II. I quickly asked for Tehachapi II as did eight others, with the remaining guys wishing to go to California Institution for Men as they were from Southern California. Then two or three days later we turned in our property and boarded a bus for Tehachapi, taking about 20 guys fresh from reception to drop off at Avenal State Prison.

It was such a relief to be riding the bus out of Wasco. I figured Tehachapi would be so much better than what I had put up with here for almost two years.

19

Avenal State Prison

This was probably one of the more pleasant bus rides I'd taken and the driver assured us that he only had two stops to make, at Avenal and Tehachapi. He was so happy about the short run, saying everyone would be in their proper places by noon. He even put on an easy rock music station and piped it through the bus.

As we began the approach to Avenal, I recognised the area, even though it was in Kings County. I'd been out here with friends hunting wild pigs. The actual town of Avenal had almost totally disappeared because of people moving away, until this prison was built, bringing in prison staff and inmates' families to revive the town. After pulling up through the prison gates, the Avenal inmates were unloaded in just a few minutes. When the bus driver assured the nine of us going to Tehachapi that we would be back on our way in about fifteen minutes, it brightened up our moods.

As we were sitting there alone, we felt comfortable talking among ourselves. Two of the other guys had previously done time at Tehachapi and were telling us about all the good things we would find there. The only bad thing about the place seemed to be the snow in winter – you had to walk through it to get to the chow hall. We were so involved in the conversation that none of us noticed a sergeant had stepped on to the bus. As soon as we did, all conversation ceased. Looking at him, I felt an ache in the pit of my stomach. He had a great big smile and sparkle in his eyes.

"Where are you guys going?" he asked us.

"Tehachapi, sir," many of us replied.

His smile widened and the ache in my stomach worsened.

"I have good news, and I have bad news," he said. "Which would you like first?"

I'd learned a long time ago that those were trick questions, so I waited.

"Well, give us the bad news first," some idiot said.

"Tehachapi is closed for intake," the sergeant replied.

"Well, what's the good news?" most of the other guys responded.

The sergeant's smile went from ear to ear. "We have nine extra beds here at Avenal, so come on down and get off the bus. You're staying," he said with a hint of glee.

This Receiving and Release unit was relatively small considering the size of the institution. There were six yards, but only two holding tanks, which could accommodate about 20 men each. The guys who had initially been sent to Avenal were in one tank and the nine of us were ushered into the other one.

My name was called out and I was directed to a telephone box-sized holding cell. One officer removed my shackles before he put me inside. Other officers were removing the shackles of the guys I'd come in with. When I asked him why I was being separated, all they would say was that I had the oldest number. It was about 9.00am and we weren't completely processed to be housed until nearly 8.00pm, at which point we were escorted to Yard 1 and given bunks in the gym. I was given the top bunk on a triple bunk set-up. Because of the exhausting day I had it wasn't long before I was fast asleep.

Next morning, I was startled awake by huge bright lights. Not knowing where I was, I threw myself out of my bunk, totally forgetting I was on the top rack. As luck would have it, all these bunks were lined up so close together that I slammed into the set next to me before hitting the floor. I crashed into it so hard that I knocked the whole set over into the next set, not only startling dozens of inmates around me but causing the guard on the podium to spill his coffee on himself.

As he and another guard made their way over to me, there was a scream. They, along with a large crowd of inmates, ran toward the common toilet and sink area. Within seconds, an alarm was sounded and the gunner on the raised walkway yelled for everyone to get back on their racks and to be quiet. More than a dozen guards and a couple of sergeants ran in. I could hear one of the sergeants questioning the two guards about when they'd last conducted a walk-through of the area.

Some inmates were whispering that someone was down. As the staff were all accounted for, that meant it was an inmate. Moments later, a guard and a nurse arrived with a gurney and within five minutes rolled it away with a body, covered from head to toe with a sheet. This could only mean one thing, that an inmate was dead. The problem would be how? If it had been a drug overdose or natural causes at least a search of the gym would be done, but if he had been stabbed then most certainly we would be on lock down. Welcome to Avenal.

We were kept on our bunks for what seemed like ages, until about 20 guards came in. In teams of two or three, they went to each bunk and all three occupants had to get down for inspection. Not only did they look at our faces and both sides of our hands, but they also made us strip naked so they could see if we had any marks that may have been caused by fighting. As they finished with each bunk set, we were allowed to get dressed and sit back on our bunks to await further instructions. I saw three guys roughly dragged out of their bunk areas, handcuffed and taken through the gym door to who knows where.

Hours later, we were told everyone would be interviewed to discover if we knew what had happened. A decision would be made about whether or not we would be on lock down.

The interviews were conducted by a number of counsellors and lieutenants. I was lucky to draw a lieutenant, who saw I'd just arrived a few hours before the killing.

"I'm guessing you don't have any knowledge of what went down or why, do you?" he said.

"I don't know what happened and I don't care," I replied. "It wasn't my business."

"Then keep it that way and it will all be good."

By the time the interviews were over, a couple more guys were taken away in cuffs. We were kept on conditional lock down for the rest of the day. We couldn't leave the gym area and, though we could go into the day room to play cards or hang out, we couldn't go to the toilet without the guard's permission and then only one at a time. Our dinner was again brought to us cold and on paper trays: some kind of noodle gravy mix with vegetables, an apple and a cup of Kool-Aid. They'd forgotten to feed us lunch so most were too hungry to complain.

The next morning after breakfast, all of us from Wasco were called out of the gym and lined up in front of the yard office. Out came a lieutenant and three guards. I could tell this lieutenant was the kind who likes to intimidate and, with his goons behind him, he probably did a good job on most inmates. I hoped he and I weren't about to butt heads, as my stay at this shit-hole had certainly not started off well and I knew it could get worse quickly.

Without warning, the lieutenant stopped in front of probably the youngest in our group.

"Your mother was a take-it-up-the-butt whore and you're here because you're a turd baby" he said.

The inmate swung on the lieutenant and clipped him on the jaw. In less than a breath, the guards had the guy on the ground, cuffed him and gave a number of kicks, including a few to the head. As the guards dragged the guy away, two more guards came out of the office to replenish the lieutenant's entourage. Then the lieutenant began speaking to us again.

I realised who this nutcase was. A few years earlier, at Pelican Bay Prison, he'd been a sergeant. He'd ordered a mentally ill inmate who had refused to shower after he covered himself in faeces, to be forcibly bathed. This took place in a large tub with scalding water and hard brushes, causing the inmate to receive severe burns and additional emotional trauma. After the investigation, the staff involved were transferred to other institutions. Apparently this sergeant got promoted and here he was – wonderful, just wonderful.

The lieutenant said that 40 percent of Avenal's population were sex offenders, mixed in with the general population inmates. I guessed the idea of telling everyone up front – they thought it would work better. He went on to say that general population inmates could walk in twos or sit down and talk in threes at a time to prevent any grouping. But the sex offenders were allowed to walk in groups of up to six for their own protection. After telling us that Avenal not only had two wire fences topped with razor wire but also had a "man-killing" electric fence between them, he finished off by formally saying, "Welcome to Avenal!"

Avenal was made up of six yards. There were three 288-man buildings on each and six converted gyms holding about 100 men each: these were the dorms for a population of around 2,200 to 2,300 at all times. There were only job assignments for around 900 to 1,000 men, and most of these were outside the fence working in the Prison Industry Authority chicken production sheds, pig farm, warehouses, or doing outside maintenance jobs for the prison.

Since there wasn't a separate Level I facility, all the Level Is lived behind the fence with the Level IIs. At initial classification, due to such few jobs being available, guys were put on waiting lists of up to two years. The classification committee was offering lifers "retirement" chronos. These stated that due to the lack of jobs, lifers could opt out of the assignment waiting list, yet they would retain all the rights of someone assigned in canteen, visiting, library and hobby privileges. Many found this great as they could work on their appeals and their tans, be on the weight pile or get better at cards. But I didn't want to sit around not working. And I could see how all the idleness would lead to people doing stupid things. I didn't want to get caught up in someone else's problem.

As I was called in before the classification committee, I'd already planned a speech. If they couldn't give me a job, I wanted a transfer. After all, I was meant to be going to Tehachapi. The committee is usually made up of a captain, a couple of counsellors, someone from the Prison Industry Authority and someone from the education department. But to my surprise, there at the table was my old boss, CJ, from my Prison Industry Authority laundry crew at California Men's Colony. She smiled and winked at me, so at least I had one friendly face in the room.

When it came to the part about assigning me, I was poised to lay out my ultimatum. But CJ spoke up, telling them how I'd worked under her supervision at California Men's Colony and was skilled in working the washers, dryers and flat iron, as well as being competent in clerical aspects. She wanted me assigned to the laundry. As it turned out, here she was the Superintendent II, in charge of the laundry, so in minutes I was told I would be moving to Yard 6, where the laundry was located. For the first time in a while, I thought things were looking up.

My assigned bunk on Yard 6 was the lower one on a two-man rack. My bunkmate was an older guy who played cards every waking minute. Because we had been told of the high percentage of sex offenders at Avenal, I made a conscious choice not to get to know him.

Over the next year, I worked at the laundry. I ignored everything I saw around me, as we would have, on average, two or three stabbings a month and fights nearly every day. A couple of guys had even been stabbed in the eye with pencils while they slept. The most unnerving incident happened when someone made a light-bulb bomb (filled with petrol) and screwed it in above someone's bunk, so when the guy turned the light on it exploded, showering him with flames and flying glass. He ended up severely burned and blinded from the bomb. I thought it was amazing that in an open dorm "no one saw anything", yet there were 20 guys living there. My life was work, weight pile and back to my bunk, which I checked every time for anything that shouldn't be there, from contraband to light bulb bombs.

One day I came back to my bunk to find not only a job re-assignment ducat, but a yard change as well. I was being moved to Yard 2. I really couldn't believe it as this was where a lot of the Youth Authority guys came when they were too violent for the juvenile facilities. 70 to 80 percent of the yard would be guys between 16 and 22, and now I, at 42, was being sent there for what – to be a babysitter?

But I packed my things and reported to the office at Yard 2 for my new bunk assignment. To my surprise, I found a lieutenant waiting for me, the one who'd been a sergeant on A Quad at California Men's Colony and had been promoted here.

"I want you as my clerk," he said. "All the clerks I have are rapists and child molesters – and I don't trust any of them. So I had you re-assigned. Hope you're not too upset."

"I just lost a job that paid me double what a clerk earns," I responded. "And now I'm on a yard full of youngsters. Not exactly where I'd prefer to be."

He used his charm. "You're getting a single bunk and can work whether hours you want, so long as the reports get done. You get full use of the word processor and copier too – you can do whatever you want with them, as long as it's not pornography. I reckon you'll be able to make a good bit of money and canteen if you choose to make sports betting tickets and copies of legal work that guys need to send to the courts."

The move wasn't as bad as I thought it might have been. I could use the weight pile, go to hobby and even help out in the mill and cabinet shop, in and around my work. And having a single bunk did help a lot. Still, because I was on a yard with a lot of young guys with little sense and way too much testosterone, fights were happening up to four times a day. It could happen anywhere: in the chow hall, library, showers, even in the chapel. For every altercation, regardless how small, I had to do an incident report for the lieutenant to submit to the warden, who in turn had to send it on to Sacramento Headquarters of CDC.

There was a report of a lifer inmate with full-blown AIDS

escaping from a secure medical wing at California Medical Facility. He had somehow got a hold of some hacksaw blades, cut through the bars on his window and, using sheets, lowered himself to the ground. Then with a pair of wire cutters, he cut the fence right beneath a tower and got away into the town of Vacaville. The story went on to say he then kidnapped a man getting into a car, drove him to a secluded spot, then raped the man, left him and drove the car to San Diego.

This caused such an uproar at Avenal that the upper command prison staff wanted to ship all of us lifers back to Level III institutions. The requests were denied by Sacramento headquarters, but not before the thought of transfers rippled through the inmate population. A riot broke out in most buildings on the yards at the same time on that day. I don't know who or what started it in my building, but coming back for lunch, I found myself in the middle of an out-and-out free for all.

My path was blocked by a guy with a knife, who was slashing at me. Doing what my military training taught me, I stepped up. So when he plunged at me again, I was able to catch his arm, then twisting his wrist around forced him to drop the knife, which I quickly kicked away. At that moment I was so angry, I snapped his wrist back to touch his forearm, hearing the tendons tearing as he screamed in pain.

But I made the fatal error of not looking behind me. I was grabbed by a big arm coming across the left side of my body, pulling me backwards into something solid. A right arm swept across my face. As it was coming back, I felt something sharp cutting into my cheek near my eye. I lifted my face in time for the cutting device to slash me across the tip of my nose instead. As the right arm left my body, I could see it was coming back for a second strike. So I slammed my head back into the person's face behind me, at the same time stomping my boot down on his right instep. He immediately let me go, at which point I started pummelling him with lefts and rights until I had him on the floor.

He was still holding his weapon in his right hand, so I stomped repeatedly on his right arm until I was sure it was broken. Taking the item from him, I headed to the bathroom sinks. I could see the tip of my nose had a big piece of meat hanging from it. I took off my T-shirt, soaked it in cold water and held it against my face to try to stop the bleeding. I looked down at the weapon I had taken. It was a tuna can lid that had been folded and placed inside an orange rind to protect the person's hand while using it. After bending the lid up some more, I threw it into the toilet and then performed medical treatment on myself for my slashed nose. The bleeding had stopped, so I gently pressed the piece of meat back into place and used a piece of Scotch tape to hold it all together.

Normally after a fight, the guards would do a body inspection to see who had been involved. But this time, since there were hundreds of inmates on multiple yards fighting, they decided it was far better to just worry about treating the most seriously injured. As there were no deaths, the guards just laughed when they saw anyone with bruises and walked by.

Within weeks, a large number of lifer inmates were placed on buses in the middle of the night, without their property and with no notice of where they were going. I was one of them. However lucky it might have been, I only went 12 miles up the road from Avenal to a place called Pleasant Valley State Prison in Fresno County.

20

Pleasant Valley State Prison

So there I was, shackled in the back of a van speeding off through the night to a destination unknown, with no idea why this was happening. No one was along for this journey with me, except for three guards. There were two up front, armed with pistols and a mini-14 locked into a bracket on the dash. The third was sitting next to me, almost on top of me. I tried to get some answers but their only response to my questions was to push and shove me. My nose was still in the process of healing, red like a cartoon character's who'd been drinking, but it was as if no one noticed. I couldn't believe this transfer was because of the riot, as I was certainly not thought to be one of the instigators – all of them were gaffed up within days of the incident and placed in Ad Seg. No, this was something else, but what?

The ride was a very short one. My mind had only just started to try to run through all possibilities, when in the field up ahead there were buildings surrounded by wire fences and bright lights. Another prison? So close to Avenal? I hadn't heard of any, but it seemed to be our destination. As we pulled up to the gate, I saw the sign "Pleasant Valley State Prison". Still not sure where we were, but knowing the Central Valley of California, and the short distance we travelled north, I figured it had to either be somewhere in Kings County or Fresno County. But Fresno didn't have any prisons.

I was walked down a long roadway, until finally we came to a heavy chained gate where two more guards waited to receive me.

"Is this him?" one of the guards at the gate asked.

No one answered.

The guard was handed what appeared to be the same envelope brought with me from Avenal. This new set of guards took me to a building about halfway across the yard. Close to it, I saw the sign above the door – Ad Seg.

Finally I was placed into a cell on my own.

"So what are your charges?" the guard asked.

"What charges?" I responded.

"Well it says here 'Out to Court Status'," he said while looking down at a sheet of paper. Then shrugging his shoulders, he walked away.

For the next four days I saw no one, except guards bringing the meal trays or letting us out to take showers every other day. Not a single one of them would engage me in conversation.

On my second day there, I spoke to a guy in a cell next to me through the vent. He said Pleasant Valley was in Fresno County, just outside the city of Coalinga. He told me the easiest way to get messages to people on the tier was to "shoot skip". To do this, you tore off a few strips of cloth from a sheet or t-shirt to make a line, 20 to 30 feet long and attached it to a bar of soap or piece of the sole of your shoe. You could then sling this under the door towards the cell you were trying to communicate with and they would toss out their line to hook on and pull it in. This was a highly skilled way of getting messages about without yelling out the door. Some guys were so proficient, they could use lines up to 100 feet long.

Finally on my fifth day, I was taken to a classification committee. An associate warden, captain, psychologist and counsellor sat at a table, while I was being held roughly by two guards.

"Do you know why you're here?' the captain asked.

I told him I didn't.

"Avenal sent you here on 'Out to Court Status', as you had charges from Fresno County."

"This is a mistake," I replied. "I've not been to Fresno since I received the life sentence I was currently serving back in 1984."

"Well we've had no information on what your charges were." He turned to the counsellor. "Why don't we have that information?"

"I don't know," was the simple response from the counsellor.

With that, the captain turned to converse quietly with the others in the room. "We'll get to the bottom of this," he said, "but as we don't know how dangerous you are, you'll be staying here in the 'Dog Pound'."

"You mean in Ad Seg?" I quickly asked.

He smiled and nodded.

Later that day, I was placed in one of the buildings on Yard D. Pleasant Valley, I found out was a Level III prison. Yard D was for miscreants and malcontents.

Over the next few months, I would learn that even though we were thought to be the "problem children", there were fewer fights on this yard than on any of the others. The one exception came about a month after I was released from Ad Seg. The prison officials decided it was too dangerous to have wooden tables and benches on Yard D, so instead they opted to build concrete ones. This wasn't entirely a bad idea, but they laid out a base form and had three feet of rebar sticking up out of it, leaving it like that for weeks. So true to form in a violent prison setting, during an altercation over a gambling debt, a guy was lifted up and dropped on the rebar, which immediately ripped through his body and impaled him. The prison's response was to tear up all the concrete slabs, rather than finish building the benches.

I had been at Pleasant Valley for almost six months without my property, which wasn't sent with inmates on "Out to Court" status. Every week, I'd been trying to get a counsellor to find out why I was here, as I hadn't been taken out to court. Finally, tired of just hanging out, as I couldn't even get a job without knowing my status, I basically forced my way in to see the CCII, the supervisor of all the counsellors. He wasn't happy with me barging in, but I told him I just wanted to know what was happening.

In typical CDC fashion, his response was for me to sit down. He said he would call the court to get my charges and case number, then I would be given a 115 disciplinary write up for harassing him and his staff. I told him that was fine, as long as it got resolved that day.

I sat there for more than 20 minutes while he spoke to someone, presumably at the Fresno County Court, providing them with my names, both John Wetmore and Morgan James Kane, and the date of the conviction I was currently serving time for. Mostly from his end, I could only hear the "Yes," "Oh," "I see," and "Uh hums" he was giving to whatever he was being told. Finally he asked the person, "Are you sure?" before hanging up the phone and telling me I could go.

"Now, where is my 115?" I asked him.

He looked surprised. I reminded him he said once he had my charges and case number I would be getting the 115. He dropped his head for a moment then looking up at me said apparently there were no charges pending.

"So why am I at your prison and without any property?" I asked. "Shouldn't you find out from Avenal?"

He called my old counsellor at Avenal to ask why they transferred me, as there was no court case against me. I watched his face get so red I thought he would explode.

"Either you come pick him up or you bring his C-File [Central File] and property immediately," he demanded, before slamming down the phone, so hard I was sure he'd broken it.

He told me it had been a ruse. Avenal had sent several lifers out to prisons in their counties of commitment on "Out to Court Status" after the lifer with AIDS had escaped from California Medical Facility. As CDC headquarters wouldn't let them do regular transfers, they pulled it off this way.

Avenal brought my C-File and property that very afternoon, and I was told I would be going to a classification committee within days. Sure enough, two days later, I was before yet another group of people.

"Well as a Level II inmate you can't stay here," said the captain running the committee. "So do you want to be returned to Avenal?"

I couldn't believe he'd actually asked that question. "I'd prefer to go back to CMC [California Men's Colony]."

I was told CMC was only accepting Level III inmates so that was out of the question. Then the CCII spoke up and offered Solano State Prison Level II as an alternative.

"Will that do?" I was asked.

Not seeming to have other options, I agreed.

The committee said I would be on the first bus they could get me on but they would assign me to work in education as a GED clerk until I transferred, which took almost a month.

Now finally out of one of the biggest screw-ups I'd seen, I could only hope I would have a more normal programme at the next place I landed. All I knew about Solano State Prison was that it was in sight of California Medical Facility and had originally been called CMF-South.

21

California State Prison, Solano

It was a chilly morning when we boarded the bus to Solano, and the shackles felt like they'd been just brought out of a cooler. Yet I could only think about how much chaos I'd left behind. From what I'd been able to learn about Solano, it was a reasonably mellow place to do time. Well, it was mellow if you were on the Level II Yards – the Level III side still had regular acts of violence. Thankfully I was Level II, a point made by the committee at Pleasant Valley and the reason for my quick transfer.

The ride was quick, and it seemed like no time until we were pulling on to the road that led to California Medical Facility, with one branch going off to the right, leading to Solano State Prison. Solano was like Wasco, Avenal and Pleasant Valley. They all have the same building design. In 1984, when building new prisons began, Solano was the first of the new style. Inmates poured pre-fab concrete and rebar walls, so that prisons could be quickly slapped together by inmate labour. It's always amazed me to learn that every prison in California had been constructed and fenced by prisoners, who even put up the razor wire that topped the fences. I've always found it to be so wrong that inmates would build their own prisons.

An inmate clerk came out and called out six names. As I wasn't one of these first six, I figured I'd be in the next group.

"The rest of you Level IIs will be temporarily house on the Level III Yards as we have no more beds on the Level II side," he said next.

"Here we go again," was my only thought.

Within fifteen minutes or so, with a bed roll under my arm, I was walking in a line with everyone else being sent to Level III Yards. One of the two guards escorting us stopped to open a gate leading to Yard 1. He called out about half a dozen names, including mine, and then gave us the instructions to go straight to the buildings we'd been assigned to. He re-locked the gate.

Luckily my building was the first on the left as we walked into the yard. Only one other inmate and I had been assigned there, so we were quickly settled in once we'd reported to the housing officer. As I was new on the yard, I wouldn't be cleared to go on until I'd been to classification committee the following day. The guard gave me 10 minutes to have a quick shower. When I came back, I noticed he'd thrown a couple of paperback books on my bunk. One was a Louis L'Amour western and the other was a fictional story about the Battle of Britain. I spent the evening reading them.

The next morning, after breakfast in my cell, I was informed that I would be going to the committee shortly. The person in charge of the classification committee wasn't a captain, although there was one in the room, a Correctional Counsellor III (CCIII) named Baskerville. I could tell by the look in Baskerville's eyes that he was a no-nonsense type of person.

"You're a Level II," he said straight away. "Why are you on my Yard, eating my food and sleeping in one of my beds?"

Of course, me being a shy and reserved person, immediately sat forwards in my chair. "Apparently the ignorant staff you have here couldn't find me a bed on Level II."

"Which one?" he asked, making matters worse.

"Take your pick, they're all idiots."

He called for a guard to take me back to my building. As I was leaving the room, I heard him speak to the other members of the committee. "Whatever it takes, get that asshole off my yard today."

About two hours later, a guard told me I was going to Level II to Yard 4 and my new dorm housing area. As I was making my bunk, I was approached by a couple of guys who asked if I'd seen somebody being escorted to Ad Seg over on Yard 1, since I'd moved over from there. It seemed that the guy who recently occupied this bunk had been snatched up by the guards for possession of tobacco and wine less than an hour before and taken straight to Ad Seg. I thought maybe this was what the CCIII meant when he said, "Whatever it takes." But since this guy may have been a friend of theirs, I saw no reason to offer up this idea.

After a couple of days, I was approached on the yard by four guys, all in their early 20s.

"So you're the one who took Jasper's bed?" said the biggest, in a rather surly tone.

"I took no one's bed," I said in a very calm voice. "I got the one assigned to me."

Apparently he wasn't too happy, as he explained that Jasper had been their connection for tobacco and wine coming over from other yards.

"So what you going to do to fix it?" he asked.

"Very happy to run a support group to help you all stop smoking and drinking," I responded.

The look in his eyes was as if someone had just turned out the lights. It took him about five minutes to answer.

"Are you making fun of me?"

"How can I make fun of a bunch of clowns?" I said, and I turned to walk away. I wasn't going to fight some kids and in any case, I was getting old. Too old to keep fighting these fights.

Within a few days I went to classification and I was given the job assignment of being the clerk for the associate warden of Level II Operations, which covered Yards 3 and 4. Though the associate warden was technically my boss, my direct boss was actually a free staff office technician called Boto.

Boto turned out to be one of the best bosses I ever had. He neither liked the way prisons were run nor how inmates were treated. He'd retired after 35 years in the US Air Force as a master sergeant. He always made sure that when officers and staff had any parties the clerks cleaned up and picked up the leftovers. He would also often bring us fresh fruit and vegetables that he grew at his house, knowing how poor our diet was.

One of the interesting things about my job was that Boto would often hand me a sealed envelope marked "Confidential" to take directly to the associate warden. The associate warden would tell me to open it and read the documents enclosed, to see if there was anything he really needed to read before I filed them away. The first time I was asked to do this I thought it was a trick. But he assured me that he cared very little for the incoherent wording often used in these documents – it always made them seem as if they were more important than they actually were.

After I'd been working for Boto for about three months, I found a computer on my desk. Boto said the associate warden had it delivered to help me develop my clerical skills to a more professional level. Within six months of taking up the job, I was given the assignment of ordering the privilege cards handed out to inmates on our yard. On the recommendations of the associate warden and Boto, I would be given the names of inmates who qualified for either a blue card or red card and I would deliver the card according to the counsellor's instructions.

Possession of these cards was quite important to inmates, as it informed staff which level of privileges the inmates were allowed to have, such as the number of packages they could receive each year, the amount of money they could spend in the canteen each month, and how often they could receive visits. This could have been an opportunity for an inmate in a position like mine to make extra cash on the side. I was often asked by other inmates if they could buy their red card as it would give them more privileges even though they weren't qualified to have them. I had to stand and say "No" to all races. I never play favourites nor can I be bought.

The hardest "No" came one day when I was approached by a group of Pacific Islanders, mostly from Tonga. They figured if I was claiming I was an Islander, I kind of owed it to them to just give up their cards as a homey. When I told the messenger this wasn't going to happen, I was told to meet the group at the back of the gym to discuss it. I would be lying if I said I wasn't concerned, as all the guys were in their early to mid-20s, and each one was taller and wider than I was. I definitely knew this time I would probably be hurt really bad. When 2.30pm came and I was getting off work, I headed off to the gym – believing my only choice would be to get off first and try to take down as many as I could before I was overwhelmed.

The gym was the only building between Yard 3 and Yard 4 that inmates from both yards could use, as this was where the hobby shop was located. It was also a housing unit for Level I inmates who didn't qualify to go outside the fences. Because of all the bunks, there were blind spots throughout the gym, so fights could occur without being seen by guards sitting at the podium. The gym guards also tended to read newspapers and magazines rather than pay attention to what was going on.

As I entered the gym door from Yard 4, I was met by a youngster, who led me back towards the shower alcove, the best fighting ground. Taking a deep breath, I stepped in, knowing it could possibly be my last. There waiting for me were 15 guys all under the age of 30. Setting my feet, clenching my fists and positioning my shoulders to give myself the best fighting position I could bring to bear, I was ready for the shit to hit the fan.

Then from behind me I heard a booming voice, followed by laughter.

"Hey, Manx Boy, didn't you learn the last time how hard an Islander's jaw is?"

With a quick glance over my shoulder, I saw Pineapple standing there. He came over and put his arm round me.

"This is the guy who broke my jaw in two places," he said, looking at the group of guys. "You can take my word, he's a true Islander. Or don't take my word and you'll have to fight us both."

One of the younger guys, who was trying to be a leader, put his hand out. "Sorry Bro, we didn't really know who you were. It's all good now."

Pineapple and some other guys invited me back to their building on Yard 3 for a cup of coffee and to catch up on where we'd been over the years. Pineapple told me he'd heard there was this white guy on Yard 4 claiming to be an Islander and who was as stubborn as hell – refusing red cards to the Pacific Islanders when they demanded them. He reckoned he only knew one person in the system stupid enough to stand up to all of them, so he thought he'd come over to check him out.

I noticed he seemed a bit smaller than I remembered and I asked him if he was feeling OK. He gave me a puzzled look, then smiled and opened up his shirt to show me a wide scar going down his chest. Around eight years ago, he'd been trying to bench about 850lbs when the bar snapped on him. Through his stubbornness, he tried to hold the bar together, which caused his pectoral muscles to rip off across his chest. Doctors had sewn and stapled them back into place, but he'd only been able to start lifting weights again a couple of years ago. He told me he was glad to see me again and that he hoped I was doing OK. He added that if I needed anything, all I had to do was send him a message.

A couple of weeks later, there was a mini-riot on the Yard 1 weight pile. More than half a dozen guys were seriously injured. One was killed when he was smashed on top of his head with a large dumbbell. The staff believed this wasn't a spur-of-the-moment incident but one that had been planned for a while, though no one was identified as the killer. The whole riot was done and dusted in less than three minutes, with all participants leaving the area, except those too injured. Within days, all the weights were removed from Solano.

It was now 1999 and time for my first parole board hearing, the one I should have had back in 1996. Since receiving the news of Mark's death, I'd been questioning my purpose if I got paroled. But I still prepared to go and fight for my freedom.

My counsellor asked if I had a paid attorney to represent me or whether I wanted the State to appoint someone. He was quite taken back when I told him I would represent myself, and asked me why.

"An appointed attorney got me in here," I replied. "So I have serious doubts one can actually try to get me out. I'm not having any dump truck getting a free lunch off me."

He was still shaking his head when I left his office.

The day of my parole hearing, I was escorted to the holding area where the hearings were held and found four other guys waiting there. Two of them had hired attorneys paid for by their families, while the other two had been appointed the same state attorney to represent them. When asked who was representing me, I said that I represent myself. They all stared at me, and I'm sure they all thought I was a nutter as few men ever went in like that. But I was confident I'd done all I needed to be given parole, I had job skills, taken self-help groups and, with the exception of the fight with Wesley Tucker 15 years earlier, had no serious write-ups. Based on what other lifers had told me, I'd ticked all the boxes. What could go wrong?

It turned out that as I had no legal representation, my hearing was moved to last. So I watched each one go in before me and, after two to three hours, come out with a stunned look on their faces – a couple were even crying. I was the only one from Yard 4 with a hearing today, so I knew nothing about these other guys. As they came by me, they would raise their hand and show fingers of how many years they'd been denied. The two with paid attorneys came out holding up five fingers. A five-year denial was the most you could be given, which was a shock to your system, especially if you'd been doing everything right. But no matter how big the shock to the person receiving it was, the shock to their family would have been worse, I'm sure.

I started waiting for this hearing at 6:30am – the board didn't begin the first hearing until 8am – and it was now 6pm. The fourth guy came out and gave me a weak smile, holding up two fingers, before being escorted away.

CHAPTER 21

"You'll get your hearing after the board has their dinner," the guard told me.

"And I've not had lunch *or* dinner," I replied.

"Hey that's the way it goes. You can always waive your hearing so you can go back to your yard to eat."

He must have been one of the stupidest guards ever.

Shortly afterwards, a tall, shapely well-dressed woman arrived at my holding tank. She told me she'd been the appointed attorney for the last two guys. As the board found out I was without legal representation, they asked her to see about representing me. I was about to decline her offer when she said, "Oh, by the way my name is Bambi." That did it, not only did I not want an appointed attorney but I certainly wasn't taking one in called "Bambi". But I chose to be very polite.

"You know nothing about my case – there'll be little chance to argue for my parole."

"You thought the attorney will help you get found suitable?" she responded. "No, we're here to try and prevent your rights from being violated."

That was the final straw.

"My rights have been violated ever since my arrest, and my defence attorney did nothing to prevent it. So thank you for your time."

The guard came for me. It was now my turn in the lion's den.

When I arrived in the hearing room, three men were whispering to each other, though they stopped the moment they saw me. The one in the centre was the board commissioner and the other two were deputy commissioners. They explained that the hearing was to see if I was suitable to be released on parole and that I wasn't a risk to society. The hearing was being recorded so I had to speak up so the mic could hear me.

"This is the initial Parole Consideration Hearing for John Wetmore."

I quickly spoke up. "No sir. My name is Morgan James Kane."

The commissioner looked down at his paperwork. "Well, it says here John Raymond Wetmore."

I pulled out the certificate with my name correction and passed it over to him across the table. He read it and then passed it to the deputy commissioner, before looking back at me.

"I've never seen anything like it," he said. "As far as I'm aware, inmates can't change their names in prison."

"But I wasn't changing my name. I just corrected it." I showed him my Abstract of Judgement, showing my true name as Morgan James Kane.

The commissioner asked the guard to remove me back to the holding tank, while they considered what had just transpired.

About 15 minutes later, the guard takes me back into the room.

"For this hearing, we're using 'Wetmore'," the board told me.

"It's simpler that way. You can always appeal if you so choose."

For the next hour and a half, they asked questions and I answered them, they asked for documents and I produced them. Then finally the guard again escorted me out while the board deliberated their decision. Sitting in the holding tank, I felt pretty confident I'd met all their requirements for parole. Half an hour later, I was taken back in for the decision.

The mood in the room gave away nothing, as they were sitting there with pleasant looks on their faces. Then the commissioner spoke.

"It's after 9pm, and I'm sure everyone wants to go home, so we'll make this short and sweet."

Well that sounded positive.

"Since you've done so much positive programming, you've made it hard for us to find a reason to deny you."

Still sounded good.

"However," the commissioner started off his next sentence, "with the political climate being what it is, and the Governor denying all parole grants, the Board has decided that to give you a parole suitability at this time, wouldn't be fair to you as it wouldn't stand." He took a breath. "The Board believes that it would be in your best interest to give you a three-year denial. By then, with any luck, there will be a different governor in office and your chance at parole will be better." He took another breath. "The Board has decided to deny you application for parole suitability on the gravity of the nature of your crime. This hearing is now closed and we wish you well."

The guard quickly rushed me out of the hearing area.

On the way back to my yard, I was trying to make sense of what had just happened. The commissioner made it sound as though denying me was for my own good and giving me a three-year denial was in my favour. So they were keeping me in prison to help me be better suited at a future parole hearing, if we had a different governor by then. Later on, I realised I'd been seriously "flim-flammed" by the board. That made me angry, as they did what was easy, rather than what was right. Again, I'd paid the price.

Even though Solano hadn't been too bad for me, I decided I would request a transfer at my post-board committee. I certainly didn't want to be here in a dorm for the next three years, preferring instead to try to get back into a cell, where I could have some peace and quiet. The following week at my post-board I did just that, and a transfer was granted. I would be going back to Folsom. Too late to change my mind, but I wondered how many there would remember me, if the troubles would start again and, if so, how soon.

22

Folsom State Prison

The ride back to Folsom was filled with dread, as I started to second-guess my decision to leave Solano. I wondered what was going through the minds of the other 20 or so guys making this trip. I could only hope that since the Aryan Brotherhood had killed Wesley, maybe I wasn't such a big issue for them any longer.

Initially I was assigned to a cell on the third tier in Folsom's Building 1. This was the same five-tier monstrosity I'd gone into back in 1984, the first time I arrived at Folsom. The only things different were that it was noisier and dirtier. The yelling and commotion of inmates running up and down the stairs showed me that either the guards didn't care or they condoned what had been happening since Folsom became a Level II prison. I knew it was very different from the Folsom I'd left and I wasn't sure who was running the place.

Remnants of the Aryan Brotherhood were few and far between and had little power, as the Skinheads were now the predominant White group on the yard. They were too busy chasing drugs and worrying about Whites who were running with the Blacks to even take much notice of me. Though on a few occasions, one would say they'd heard I used to be something in the past. Most of these Skinheads hadn't even been born when I first came to prison.

I'd been assigned to Vocational Janitorial I, a course that taught me how to mop and wax concrete floors and dust prison bars. The staff supervisor and instructor told me my job would be to sweep and mop the one-quarter section of the first tier, twice a day, right after Work Line in the morning and after Yard went out in the afternoon.

I took every opportunity to go back in to my cell between each cleaning period. My cell mate, Dan, had ironically known of me at California Men's Colony when he was there, though we never met. I told him I could make things out of pieces of wood. One day he brought back from work some glue, string, different grits of sandpaper and small jars of paints, as well as around 100 lolly sticks he'd picked up of the yard and washed. Giving them to me, he said he hoped I could use it all to make something. I began by making miniature motorcycles, about six inches long. These turned out to be a big hit on the yard, and I would sell them for about $10 each, usually paid for in the canteen. So when I wasn't at work, I would be in my cell hobbying.

About three months into my job, my supervisor came looking for me. He stood at my cell door with his hands on the bars.

"Why aren't you at work?" he asked.

"I'd done my job," I replied. The guards don't like having lots of inmates out there running around, so I came back in here. I'm easy enough to find."

He didn't believe me, and went to ask the guard, who backed up my story – that I did my job as instructed and then went back to my cell. My supervisor told me this would have to change and, in a huff, he left. I continued to hobby.

A week later, I was told I would no longer be a student in Vocational Janitorial I, but a clerk instead. I reported to the supervisor's office to start my new job. The lead clerk told me I had to listen to what he had to say as well.

"If you're not paying me the eight cents an hour, then you've nothing to say," I said to the lead clerk.

This didn't go down with him very well. And from then on, if I needed any help, this other clerk wouldn't assist me at all. So I had to get on the best way I could and try to figure things out for myself.

One day, while the other clerk was at a medical appointment, the supervisor needed some documents off this clerk's computer. I had no access so the supervisor, using his password, unlocked this computer for me. I noticed this clerk had a very specific way of naming his saved documents – so that only he knew what they were. Once I'd printed off what the supervisor wanted, I set about changing all the parameters on as many document files as I could, and then saved them. Finally with all the files still open, I did a hard shutdown.

When I came to work the following day, I found the other clerk almost in tears as he was trying to fix all his files.

"What did you do to my computer?" he asked me.

"Well, since you didn't want to teach me anything, I had to go with a trial-by-error method. So I made the errors and now you're dealing with the trials. To stop any problems in future, your might want to share some of your knowledge and experience. Then we can work as a team. I'm not someone to be played with – I never learned how to play nice."

The next morning, he'd made us both cups of coffee and had set out some honey buns so we could talk.

"I'm used to having to work with really stupid guys," he said. "I now realise you're not one of them. So I'll teach you anything you want to know – just ask."

This working relationship got better over the next year until I left to become a hobby clerk.

It was now 2000, and I seemed to be getting on all right on the yard, with no threats. From what I could tell, no one was even speaking much about me. I met a guy who worked for Vocational Janitorial III, which operated in Building 3, and it turned out he was British. He told me there was this organisation in London called Prisoners Abroad, which provided support to British nationals serving time in prisons around the world. He suggested I write to them, as they should be able to help me with the problems of getting officials to recognise me as a British citizen. So I did contact them, though I wasn't really expecting much as I'd never received much help from authorities of any kind. Just days before I heard back from them, the guy was picked up by Immigration to be deported back to the UK.

Initially Prisoners Abroad wasn't able to give me a lot of help, as I had no registered birth. All I had was a copy of my 1983 jail log and a 1990 letter from the Fresno Public Defenders. This letter confirmed that my original baptismal certificate had been given to the San Francisco British Consulate in 1983. I and Prisoners Abroad wrote to the consulate, but they claimed to know nothing about it. Still, Prisoners Abroad sent me their newsletter and books about what I would face when I came home to the UK. These things alone were so important, as I still wasn't receiving letters from anyone – no family and no friends, as they had all fallen by the wayside many years before.

The hobby clerk job turned out to be only a half-day position as the manager was in fact the warehouse supervisor too. For part of the day, he had to bring new clothing into Folsom for distribution, so he gave all his workers the option to either go to the yard in the morning or work in the clothing room. If we chose the latter, we would get paid the same as if we were working in hobby, a big 22 cents an hour. I chose the clothing room/hobby shop option, as it enabled me to make $1.76 a day. This may not seem like much, but I had no outside support. Along with my earnings from the sale of my little model motorcycles, I could buy some comforts from the canteen.

Because of my hobby job, I was assigned to Building 5 where all the hobby workers lived. These cells had no bars on their doors; instead, they were heavy steel doors with holes drilled in to provide some ventilation – as someone would picture a dungeon. Because of this move, I gained a new celly who also did a lot of hobby work. His speciality was inlaying gold wire into thin granite pendants, usually forming the Folsom State Prison logo. These were very much desired by the correctional staff. Though he and I tolerated each other, we never became anything close to becoming friends. When I came back to our cell one day and found him doing inlay work on some flip blade "buck knives" for a guard who'd brought him these contraband weapons, I knew it was time to move out.

I bribed the housing clerk $20 to move me into my own cell in Building 5. Through my contacts in different maintenance shops, I was able to pay to have a bigger, deeper sink put in my cell. I also had extra electric plugs and better lights installed, as well as a work counter for my hobby. As with most prisons, money could buy things to make life more comfortable, and I was able to make extra money through the things I made. But I couldn't become too comfortable.

My job only lasted for about six months before the hobby shop was shut down. When laying a new floor for the counsellors' offices above the shop, workers discovered a trapdoor right above my clerk's desk. This trapdoor was used in the early part of the 20th century when hangings were performed at Folsom. A female counsellor's chair had actually stood on it. The trapdoor had been concealed only with a thin piece of plywood – and it was still fully functional. The female counsellor was so traumatised by this fact that she actually transferred from Folsom to another prison.

The big change over the years was that the Skinheads were now more in charge than the Whites at Folsom. They seemed to call the shots, especially if they'd come from the Youth Authority facilities. Many of them had Hispanic surnames, and you could tell they were bi-racial. If a guy named Sanchez-Martinez covered in Nazi tattoos told you he supported "White Power", you'd think he was having an identity crisis. But it didn't seem to be a problem – maybe because in the last 20-plus years, race wasn't considered as restrictive out in the free world as it was in prison. As long as they left me alone, I didn't care what they did.

When the hobby shop closed, I was reassigned to China Hill. Very few lifers were given this opportunity. First I was given a small barren patch to work with, but after about a month I got promoted. The inmate who was supposed to take care of the greenhouse and raise the flags every morning decided to drag them through the dirt in front of the guards. He was immediately reassigned to a dump job on the lower yard, which meant I was given these responsibilities instead.

China Hill was a place of peace and solitude. Its main purpose at the time was to grow fruits and vegetables that could be donated to community food programmes, such as food banks, soup kitchens and senior citizens' centres. Knowing that our produce was going to such good causes made a lot of men feel better about themselves, and they would try to produce as many crops as they could. Among the things we grew were spinach, cauliflower, broccoli, onions, bell peppers, tomatoes, squash and an assortment of melons. The guards on the Hill with us were some of the most humane I'd met in the system. Not only would they bring in packs of seeds, but, on occasion, the food banks would send back cookies or cake with the delivery guard – these items were divided among the inmates who'd produced the most food. This incentive brought about some welcome healthy competition. It was one of the best jobs I'd had since coming to prison.

Finally, after about eight months on China Hill, I was reassigned back to the hobby shop, which was now open again. The hobby shop was significantly smaller and served as somewhere for ordering materials, picking up orders and dropping off finished items. The renovation had removed all the equipment the inmates used to make their items.

CHAPTER 22

Everything had to be done out of your cell, so the type of hobby and tools allowed was drastically limited. Luckily for me, I was still able to do my motorcycle model making, as I could keep the modelling knives, sandpaper, glue and paint in my cell.

One of the Folsom inmates was Cameron Hooker. I was told he'd kept a girl in a box under his bed. I hadn't heard of him before so went to do some research. I found out that Cameron Hooker had been convicted of multiple counts of sexual assault. In 1977, he and his wife Janice picked up Colleen Stan, a hitchhiker. Colleen thought this would be a safe ride as Janice was holding a baby in her lap. But this began a seven-year nightmare of torture and sexual abuse, involving everything from being locked in a box under a bed to being hung up by her arms from the ceiling with a box around her head to prevent light, sound and fresh air from entering. The whole affair was pretty sordid.

Cameron had been at Folsom for a good few years before I met him. You'd expect him to have problems with the Aryan Brotherhood as he'd been convicted of sex crimes, but in fact they really liked him and even protected him. He would spend hours on the yard sharing stories of his sexual escapades to a very entertained crowd of his admirers. Outside of my job I had very few dealings with him, mainly because I wanted it that way. But he did work in the prison canteen, which meant I would see him there every month.

In 2002, I appeared before the parole board for the second time. This hearing was even shorter than the first. There were only two board members, both women, a commissioner and deputy commissioner. They stated that the "gravity of the nature of the crime" was sufficient cause to deny me, giving me a further two-year denial, then wished me well. That was that, and life went on.

By 2003, I became the watch commander's clerk. This job was very much like the one I had at Solano. One of my tasks involved ensuring the processing of the transfers of inmates via a CDC 135 form was done correctly. So I knew a week ahead who was going to be transferred and to where. I also had the responsibility of putting together the "Special Transports", which could be anything from medical runs, court runs or the all-important protective custody runs.

In 2004, Cameron Hooker was brutally attacked at the prison library by a Skinhead who was said to be distantly related to his victim. Cameron was deemed in need of a transfer so was sent to his current prison, Corcoran SATF, for his protection. It was my pleasure to do the paperwork that got him transferred, because I believe his life of luxury due to his Aryan Brotherhood protection would now be a thing of the past.

One day, I returned to my cell after work to find my tier being mopped by three guys. They hadn't placed any "wet floor" signs up, as we'd been taught in Vocational Janitorial, and they had way too much water down, which made it extremely slippery. I was trying to get to my cell door, as I needed my celly to pass me my shower kit and towel. I had to cross the tier to actually reach it. Being mindful of my steps, I began to cross, watching where I placed my feet. All of a sudden, I heard the sound of rolling caster wheels and, before I could react, found myself falling to the floor. At just the right moment, one of the guys had rolled the mop bucket at me, catching me right behind the left knee, causing it to buckle. I could see the three guys trying to get at me: one had a club and another was holding a weapon that I couldn't quite make out in his right hand.

I was finally able to get to my feet by my cell door. With my celly looking out, the guy with the club attacked, hitting me about a dozen times on my shoulder, side and legs, attempting to get me back on the ground. I stepped up on to the small ledge in front of my cell to get my footing. Then I backhanded my attacker, causing him to step back and fall. The third guy opened a bottle of liquid and started to throw it, just as the guy with the weapon slashed at my wrist.

Grabbing the guy's arm after he'd cut me, I realised he had a razor blade fixed to a toothbrush handle. Though not as dangerous as an actual knife, it could still cause a serious injury, especially if it slashed at my face. As I slung him away, I could feel fresh wetness hit me in the back of my head and heard it landing against my door. Then I heard my celly yell out something was in his eyes. I turned to face the guy who'd thrown the liquid, while at the same time telling my celly to wash out his eyes.

Just as I started to reach for the guy, I felt a sharp pain in the inside of my left arm. Looking down, I saw the guy with the razor had again slashed me, causing a longer and deeper cut. Now I found myself facing both the guy with the club and the guy with the razor. I had only one option. I did a quick hop off my door ledge, hoping I wouldn't slip, and made my way to the mop bucket, where I grabbed up the metal mop wringer and started to swing it.

The two attackers were right next to each other. So when I hit the one with the club, he fell into the other one and they both lost their footing. I was able to move on them and hit them a couple of times before turning to give my attention to the third. I was in for a surprise. He was being held by a couple of guys I'd had casual contact with at different prisons over the years. One had been a friend of my driving partner, Ted, at California Men's Colony.

"We only just heard you were to be hit today, and were coming to warn you," the guy said. "Sorry we didn't get here earlier. What do you want us to do with this guy?"

"Toss him on the floor with the other garbage," I responded.

Ted's companion gave the guy a couple of good punches before tossing him down next to the ones I'd handled with the mop wringer.

"I won't just remember your faces," I said to the three guys on the floor. "I'll be pointing you out to others on the line. And using any juice I have – canteen, laundry or housing

– I'll make all of your lives miserable. Any sense you may move on me again, and I'll seriously damage you first."

I checked on my celly. Luckily, they'd just thrown soapy water, so he wouldn't have any permanent damage. I got him to pass me out an elastic bandage so I could wrap my arm before I went to shower. By the time I turned back, the three were gone, though the two who came to help were still there, telling me they'd added their own warning.

It turned out that these guys had heard of my problem with the Aryan Brotherhood 20 years earlier. They thought getting some "stripes" by taking me down would earn a reputation with some of the real Aryan Brotherhood in Pelican Bay Security Housing Units. But they made this attempt without getting approval from a Skinhead shot-caller. That, and the fact it failed, even with the element of surprise, caused them to become targets within their own group. Within a month, I had seen their names on transfer lists heading out to other prisons. Word was, they let an old man, twice their age, beat the three of them, so the Whites saw them as an embarrassment.

Within a few months, my name came up to transfer out. The watch commander said if I wanted to stay he would personally pull me off the bus. But I told him I didn't like the way the yard was changing, and that the change might be good as at some point all Level IIs had to be gone. He arranged for me to go to Deuel Vocational Institution Lifer

Dorm. I had no idea what that was. All I knew was that Deuel Vocational Institution was no longer a mainline prison. Instead, it had become a reception centre, with only a small mainline to run essential operations.

In the past, Deuel Vocational Institution had carried the title of "Gladiator School". I was getting too old to have to keep fighting.

23

Deuel Vocational Institution

The staff at Deuel Vocational Institution seemed almost happy to see us, bringing over some apples and cartons of milk, still cold. They told us dinner would be arriving soon. It took about an hour to get us processed and, true to their word, a food cart arrived. It turned out to be enchiladas, beans, rice, salad and cake – not the tastiest, but it was warm and filling.

A guard took us to our wing, walking us down the first tier in C-Wing. He stopped at one cell then another, leaving just one of us at each. Finally we got to Cell 110 – mine. I couldn't believe it. This was the same cell I'd lived in all those years back here at Deuel Vocational Institution.

My celly was sitting up on the top bunk with his face buried in a law book. He didn't even look up when the door opened.

"Well, I guess we're in here together," I said after a minute.

He slowly lowered the book to where I could just see his eyes. "I'll be going to L-III tomorrow," he said, and then went back to his reading.

With that little introduction over, I set about making up my bunk and called it a night.

At about 5:30am, I heard a commotion out on the tier and jumped up to look out the cell window. There were hundreds of guys in orange jumpsuits, milling around and talking. But as no one could hear anyone else, it was just a rise and fall roar as they tried to get heard. I looked back at my celly, who was again reading a law book and seemed not to notice what was going on.

"We go to chow once they get them all back in their cells," he said. "It can take a while though."

Since he'd spoken first, I decided this would be the right opportunity to introduce myself.

He again peered over his book and muttered that his name was Samuel. Giving nothing more, he went back to his reading.

Finally the cell door popped and off to chow we went, which was sadly not as good as dinner. Within minutes of getting back to our cell, a guard showed up at the door with a cart to move my celly to L-III. I realised he had 20 boxes of property, mostly filled with books and paperwork – I'd never seen so much.

When I appeared before the classification committee, they informed me that I would be going up to L-III as soon as a bed was available and that I was being placed on the Prison Industry Authority list for a job. I'd heard that L-III inmates had keys to their cells, but there were no toilets or sinks in them, meaning all inmates up there had to use communal-style facilities.

At L-III, I was sent to Cell 345. Samuel was up on the top bunk.

"I saved you the bottom bunk and got you a pillow," he said, climbing down. "Are you afraid of wasps? We've got some outside the window."

"No, everything from spiders to tigers and the occasional dragon, I can deal with," I replied.

He opened the window and walked out of the cell, and I then heard the key locking the door. Suddenly there wasps flying all around. Samuel said he'd be back in a minute. I quickly shut the window, picked up a magazine off the desk and rolled it up, swatting down the wasps. Soon there were no wasps left.

Samuel returned and unlocked the cell.

"What the hell did you think you were doing?" I yelled.

He looked at me quite innocently. "I'm allergic to bee and wasp stings. I couldn't open the window in case they stung me. I hoped you'd fix the problem."

I realised something about Samuel was different. I later ended up clearing out the wasp nest in our window so he could have it open without any concerns.

Samuel had a number of quirks. He would sometimes grasp his hands and grimace like he was having a terrible bowel movement when out walking in the unit or even in the chow line. I would come back to the cell and see him rocking back and forth as if having a fit, though he would stop quickly once he knew I was there. He was drenched with sweat afterwards.

Many guys in the unit thought he was crazy, but I knew there was something else going on. So about a week after us being cellies, I finally asked him.

He contemplated for a moment before answering. "I've got Asperger's syndrome, a type of autism."

Samuel was very intelligent, a member of MENSA with an IQ rated above 160. He could play four games of chess against four other guys at the same time and rarely ever lost a game. He had a Master's degree in Business Administration and a great memory when it came to legal cases and changes in the law. He had a job in the law library and would often help guys file paperwork, for divorces, child custody and even writs against parole board denials. At no time did he ever charge for helping. It vexed him that the writs were always denied, as the Governor of California still had his "no parole" policy in play.

Within a couple of weeks, I was working at the furniture factory cutting out and sanding table and chair pieces, after which I was offered a job as the accounting clerk in the office – 75 cents an hour rather than 35 cents an hour, so how could I say no? Besides, I wouldn't be covered in sawdust every day.

My boss was a woman from India. It turned out she liked the fact I picked up the job so quickly and that I had a good memory for parts and materials we ordered and the companies we dealt with, even if only used occasionally. The joke in the office was that I was the BUS (back-up system), should the computers go down.

In November 2005, I went to my third parole board hearing as it had been two years since my last one at Folsom. Though this was still done by just a commissioner and deputy commissioner and took about three and a half hours, the outcome was the same, except this time I was denied because they thought I needed to do some "reflection on my life" and figure out where I thought it should go. Then after they gave me a two-year denial, they wished me well, yet again.

By now I was busy at my job and, when not at work, I was in the hobby shop, doing woodwork, mostly carvings. There was something very calming about working with my hands, and the fact I could take a piece of wood and bring something beautiful out of it was quite rewarding. I often made jewellery boxes with intricate one-of-a-kind designs. As I had no one to give them to, I would give them to guys who had wives and daughters, so they could brighten up their day.

24

Finally in 2006, the lady at Prisoners Abroad wrote for about the fifth or sixth time asking me if I wanted a pen pal in the UK. I'd told her that I intended to give up my US citizenship, which I believed I'd gained when Dr Wetmore adopted me, and would return to my birth country when my sentence was over. I'd previously politely refused her offer, feeling I didn't want anyone doing my time with me. This time it was different though, as she very firmly pointed out that one day I would be returning to a country I had no memory of and it would be useful if I had someone to help me learn about what I might face. I agreed that if she could find me someone, I would write to them.

Soon after I received a letter via Prisoners Abroad from a woman who said she'd been asked to write to me. She was born in London and was a grandmother. She told me I could tell or ask her anything but I'd better not lie, as she'd worked for 24 years for the British government, part of the time investigating benefit fraud. I was taken back at how blunt she was. But I immediately wrote back and said, "All right, I won't lie to you, but you're not going to like me."

This was the start of a 12-year letter-writing friendship, in which we would exchange over 645 letters. Though I never lied to her she discovered that some things I told her had, in fact, been lies told to me when I was growing up. She was instrumental in helping me to prove my British identity and citizenship.

Now I had someone in Britain who was able to explain things to me. At times, I'm sure it wasn't easy for her. At her request, I sent her copies of my board denials. She couldn't find the grounds for them, especially when I'd been participating in the programmes they'd asked of me. I sent her all the chronos I was given, showing my successful completion of them.

Deuel Vocational Institution at this time was really starting to change. CDC created the Special Programming Unit (SPU), which would take all the sex offenders, gang dropouts, guys who owed drug debt, homosexuals/transgenders and snitches, lumping them all together. The prison always had the reputation of a lot of violence, though violence on the mainline had been almost nothing since I'd arrived back, except the occasional fist fight. Now on the reception side all hell was about to break loose, especially in the Special Programming Unit, where the mixture was so volatile that new gangs were starting to come into being. We were hearing about groups called The Northern Riders, Gay Boy Gangsters and Deep Throat Locas, the last two being formed for the protection of guys whose sexuality might not fit the norm in the Special Programming Unit. Every week, there were reports of fights, stabbings with sharpened plastic toothbrushes or broken glass pieces from the windows being used. There had even been a couple of deaths.

Sometime in May 2007, my pen pal suggested I think about requesting a prison transfer under the International Transfer of Prisoners Treaty. She was aware of the overcrowding and worsening conditions of US prisons, and believed I stood a better chance of being paroled if I was in a UK prison. From then on, I started to talk more about my origins so I made my initial attempts to get transferred back to the UK. Unfortunately they seemed to go nowhere.

Sadly my boss got a better job working in the Deuel Vocational Institution Records department. My new temporary supervisor had only been the staff aide. She had no accounting experience and hadn't even graduated from high school. Yet now, with her new-found power, she became the expert in everything, though all mistakes she made she blamed on others.

During lunch, she often held what was known among the inmates as her "Boobs and Bible" study. She would talk to guys about the bible, but not before undoing a couple of buttons on her top so her cleavage showed. I guess this was to get the guys to focus on something while she preached. It seemed effective, as she always had two or three guys listening. She had, I soon discovered, a real strange attitude about a lot of things. She liked to quote bible scriptures, but would get them wrong. There was one instance when she was doing an impromptu "bible study" with the two inmate porters.

"And that's when they stoned Jesus," she said.

The other clerk in the room, who was Jewish, looked at me. "Jesus was never stoned," he said to her.

"Well your people killed my Saviour," she replied, to his surprise.

After that, both he and I stayed quiet about her remarks.

She'd also made the comment on many occasions that she could never fully trust anyone who wasn't a real American. I told her I was born in the UK but, because CDC hadn't accepted that and the fact that I sounded American, she believed I was only teasing her.

I continued with the programme and stayed out of trouble while preparing for my next board, which was scheduled for November 2007. Again, I felt I'd complied with all the requests by the previous parole board panel but this one gave me yet another two-year denial and wished me well.

At this time, most lifers believed that less than 18 of us would be freed while still alive, and that our only hope was that the legislation changed or the courts would break the state governor's power. So I doubled my efforts to get a transfer back to the UK.

By January 2008, one of the Immigration Customs Enforcement (ICE) agents, who regularly visited the prison, told me that as I wasn't a Mexican I could pass as an American, and no one would question it so I should stop trying to transfer. This encouraged me even further, and in early March I again put in my transfer application, this time taking the precaution to send the letters to both the CA Prison Authorities and to the British Consulate by certified post. Finally I got confirmation on 3 April 2008 that in the UK National Offender Management Service had started to process my application for transfer.

I hadn't heard any word from our consulate but finally, on 13 April, I did get to speak to them via a phone call. When I got back to my cell, I found it had been searched and papers had been removed, including some of the letters I'd received from my pen pal. None of the officers would admit to who had turned my cell over, and no receipt was left for the items they took. But other inmates told me S and I (Security and Investigation) had been in my cell. The only good thing about this was that they only had copies of my pen pal correspondence, as we worked out a system where the letter I received from her was returned with my reply. By this time, the constant cell searches had forced me to send copies of my important documents to my pen pal for safe keeping.

On 16 April 2008, everything would start to change for me. I was notified that the supervisor in Inmate Records had done a review of my C-File and discovered that CDC had been ordered to "correct" my name to Morgan James Kane back in October 1990, almost 18 years earlier, but hadn't. On the 17 April, she immediately issued me a new ID card under Morgan Kane and notified the US Department of Justice about the correction.

Only seven days later on 24 April, officials from three federal agencies – ICE (Immigration Customs Enforcement), NCIS (Naval Criminal Investigative Service) and FBI (Federal Bureau of Investigation) all showed up to see me. Apparently they'd been looking for me since they had received a 14-page affidavit from Dr Wetmore (after his death in 1996) that told them I was illegally in the US, serving in the military under the false identity he'd given me. He'd included over 70 supporting documents. But since he told them I was being placed in prison under my true name of Morgan James Kane, when I'd been under John Raymond Wetmore all my life, they hadn't been able to find me. They questioned me for about four hours and asked me about Dr Wetmore's activities and who he knew, to which I had to explain that I really didn't know much and, at best, didn't care. This didn't sit well with them.

I'd been sitting in a chair on the far side of the table with my hands in my lap, so they thought I was handcuffed. That is, until the FBI agent, getting tired of the fact I wasn't giving them straight answers, threaten to come over and knock me out of the chair. I brought my hands above the table and they saw I wasn't restrained. He yelled out, "He's not cuffed, he's not cuffed," which brought the guard into the room.

I explained to the guard that the FBI agent had threatened to knock me out of my chair. The guard was about 70 and six inches shorter but looked at the FBI guy and told him that I was his responsibility and no one was knocking me out of a chair on his watch. That in itself was a pleasure to see. Shortly after that, the federal agents left, telling me they were launching an investigation into my national status. Before the Immigration Customs Enforcement agent left, he said, "If all of this is true, I'm not happy how you got here, or how you've been able to stay without being found out. I certainly don't like that you've tasted the fruits of America and now you want to leave."

To my surprise, on the 28 April, just a mere four days later, I was served an immigration detainer, with a box checked that said, "Deportation or removal from the United States had been ordered." It also stated my nationality to be "United Kingdom". I was delighted to say the least; finally I had proof that I wasn't an American and I was being ordered to be sent "HOME".

Now with this documented proof in hand, I couldn't wait to show people who'd doubted that what I said was true. But the responses weren't what I expected. Many guys I'd known for years suddenly stopped speaking to me and avoided me, as if I had something contagious. The biggest surprise came when I went to work and showed my boss that what I told her about not being an American was, in fact, true. She sent me to the manager of Prison Industry Authority.

"I demand he's removed from this job, as I can no longer trust him," she stated to the manager and others present. "He's one of them, not one of us."

It sounded ridiculous and I thought no one would take her seriously, but how wrong was I? The next day I was unassigned from my job. First I was placed in the bakery, which meant I went from a .75 cents-an-hour job to a .08 cent-an-hour one, but then within a few days I was moved to a first watch porter job (10pm to 6am), which had no pay.

I was no longer facing enemies wearing inmate blues, but those who wore uniforms or civilian clothes. It was the staff I had to watch out for, and they were far more dangerous, as they could put chronos in my C-File. This could cause me problems at the parole board, particularly if placed in the "Confidential" section, which I couldn't review. American pride was almost like a disease. To have someone like me who didn't want to be an American, even though I'd lived here most of my life, was hard for them to understand. This was evident when my mail from the UK was being delayed, both out going and in coming, or not being delivered at all. Then there was the increased frequency in which my cell, hobby locker and I were being searched. The upsides to this change in status were being called Kane not Wetmore, and that the Paisas (Mexican nationals) started to come to me for help as they now saw I had immigration issues. Of course now the Whites were really confused, so to most them I was "dead" and not to be helped at all, which of course was fine with me.

It took time to get staff and inmates to accept calling me by my correct last name, though many had called me Morgan over the years. Not a day went by when I didn't get asked the question, "Why did you change your name?" I had to point out that CDC had strict rules that no inmate could change their name while in prison; this was, in fact, a point used when inmates converted to Islam and wanted to take an Arabic name. This still didn't stop staff feeling I'd somehow got one over on the system. But all I'd finally accomplished was to get the system to follow its own rules.

It was months before I finally received a visit from the British Consulate in San Francisco. They seemed to be very concerned for my situation until they asked to see my birth certificate, which I didn't have. I did mention I'd been told they'd been sent my baptism certificate back in 1983, to which they claimed ignorance. They left with the promise they would help get me home, but it would be quite a while before I would hear from them again – and then it would be different people who really knew nothing about me.

In November 2008, there was another blow to the efforts

of lifers trying to get paroled, when legislature was passed called Marcy's Law, something touted as the Victim's Bill of Rights. It increased the amount of time we could be given as board denials. Quite simply, a one-year denial was now three years, a two-year denial was five years, three years was seven years, four years was 10 years and a five-year denial was 15 years. Try to imagine going to a board and coming out with a 10 or a 15 year denial; that, in itself, would be spirit-breaking, particularly if you'd already served 25 years or more.

Around the time of this legislature being passed, I found myself being placed in Ad Seg. As I'd been working as a first watch porter, my days were free, so I'd been asked by the Muslim imam, about a year earlier, if I would help his clerk by working as a volunteer in the inter-faith chapel. My job was to type out unlock lists for inmates in reception, so they could go to religious programmes of faiths such as Buddhists, Wiccans, Mormons and Jehovah's Witnesses. What I didn't know was that the head chaplain, who preached that the earth was only 6,000 years old and that Satan had put fossils into the rocks to confuse us, running the protestant chapel had been purposefully preventing these requests from being processed. When he turned the responsibility for them over to the imam, he thought that as he was Muslim he would also deny them.

But the imam was a man of honour and felt that everyone had the right to follow the faith that called to them so he turned in every list I presented to him. Right after Thanksgiving 2008, I was cuffed up by two guards and placed in Ad Seg, accused of stealing a cupboard lock in the Inter-Faith Chapel. I spent 10 days in there, before being found "not guilty" and released back to my cell, though I was banned from going to any chapel of religious programme without the head chaplain's permission.

This experience inspired me to do a drawing that I called "Nowhere Man". I sent it to Prisoners Aboard and it was entered in the Koestler Awards. It was so well received that it was displayed at the Royal Festival Hall in London and purchased by somebody who saw it. This actually would be the first of many art or woodwork pieces of mine that would win awards. I even had four more pieces displayed in the Royal Festival Hall. Luckily for me, all mention of my trip to Ad Seg was removed per CDC rules so wasn't available for future parole boards to see or use against me.

Two chaplains (the imam and the Catholic deacon) continued to show me kindness and support, though they had to do it in subtle ways to avoid raising the wrath of the head chaplain, who also held the purse strings to the money needed by each faith to purchase religious materials.

In early 2009, my pen pal notified me that she'd discovered the woman I believed to be my mother – Moya Iris Kane – had actually been called Martha Virginia Boswell and had used my mother's identity. My pen pal got hold of my mother's birth certificate and discovered she was nearly 15 years older than Martha. She did a whole family work up, even to the fact that my father had filed for divorce a month before I was born.

In August 2009, I was informed that my military service record was being taken away on the grounds that I'd served under the "false identity" of a US citizen – John Raymond Wetmore. They laid out their reasons as follows:

1. You were born in the UK and are a British citizen.
2. You entered the United States illegally.
3. You continued to remain in the United States illegally, using the name and social security number of John R. Wetmore, a US citizen.
4. You knowingly and under false pretences enlisted in the US Navy, using illegally procured identification documents.
5. You volunteered for training (Hospital Corpsman/ FMF) and service deployment (Vietnam, Spec Ops, Provost Marshal) allowing you access to sensitive and/or classified materials.

It was strange that they hadn't realised the identity I was being accused of taking was the one given to me by Dr Wetmore. They hadn't assimilated the information he'd written into his statement – that he'd tried to get me enlisted into the US Air Force. Somehow they had in their minds that as a one-year-old child coming across the Canadian/US border, I had hatched a plot to be carried out 17 years later!

Sadly, the letter went on to say that not only were they taking my service record, but all my medals, ribbons and citations. I was a "Criminal Alien and Undesirable", leaving me with the threat of prosecution under the Patriot Act and the Anti-Terrorism and Effective Death Penalty Act of 1996, if I ever subsequently tried to apply for any military benefits or the 70 percent disability pension I'd been awarded. I was also notified that I had a lifetime ban from returning to the US or any of its territories.

The reality set in during my fourth parole board hearing in October 2009. I was addressed as Kane rather than Wetmore.

"Morgan James Kane – that's a cool name. How did you come by that?" the Fresno County District Attorney representative said.

"My mom gave it to me," I responded.

I could tell by the looks on the board members' faces that they didn't like my response at all. This hearing, I'd expected to get a three-year denial as that was the lowest I could get, but they gave me a five-year one, and added insult to injury by saying that it was really still just the two years I'd already been receiving, then wished me well. This time they didn't even ask me to do anything for my next board. I was certain this was because I'd beaten them into giving me my name back, and proved I was British.

Within six months, the opportunity came up to work at the reception of the prison in the mental health department. I would be the clerk doing the initial call sheets on the inmates who'd arrived the day before, so they could be evaluated by one of the psychologists and, if necessary, set up for any mental health concerns that were identified. The job enabled me to see the types of people who were coming in and to get an idea of what was happening in society. What I found was a whole generation that seemed to have no purpose, except to use drugs and party; not one I spoke to had a single thought about getting a job, having a family and being a productive member of their community. In fact, they seemed to have no respect for themselves or even their mothers – I found this quite strange, as when I'd first come to prison saying anything about a guy's mother would start a fight.

As time went by, I developed such a good rapport with the mental health staff that I was allowed to provide the newly arrived guys with books, paper and envelopes, which I knew were hard to get on their wings. More importantly, I became an ear for the inmates who needed to talk but were afraid to say something to one of the psychologists. Their good feedback meant soon I was invited to pass on some of what I'd learned over 26 years. One of the bits I always shared was how they could make themselves less desirable to the gangs. I would explain that if you were always reading and learning, gangs tended to leave you alone as the leaders didn't want anyone smarter than them around. I got to see many of those who followed my advice go home when they were supposed to, and some even stayed out and found better pursuits to follow.

Over in England, there was a push going on by my pen pal and people at Prisoners Abroad, especially my case worker, Matt. They were doing all they could to get me recognised by the British government and the British consulate. It became important for me to stay out of trouble so I wouldn't ruin anything they were working on. This became increasingly hard as I was still being harassed by guards and inmates for being British, though I sounded American. I would come back to my cell to find our property tossed about, which only distressed my celly. Many times, important papers, letters and even photographs were taken, never to be returned. I had no recourse, as no one would tell me which guard did it. Sometimes I would find derogatory writing or pictures taped to the door. One, in particular, was an English Bulldog being hung and the words "Go Home Lobsterback" and "We hate you Redcoat." The harassment picked up in the days before 4 July, their Independence Day.

Besides my celly, a few guys had my back, and didn't like the sneaky things being done to me. One of those guys was called Wolf. Before coming to prison, he'd ridden with a motorcycle club in Oakland, California. To say he was someone not to mess with is an understatement, as he'd been convicted of killing and decapitating a man who he believed owed him money for drugs and had disrespected him. It was reported that when the police arrived at his house, they found him kicking the man's head about his yard. He was a proud member of his motorcycle club and refused all suggestions by parole boards to disassociate himself from them. In prison, he carried himself with all the pride and swagger that an Outlaw Biker Patch-Holder would be expected to do.

He continued to use drugs and fight regularly until about 2011 when he became ill with hepatitis C and sclerosis of the liver. He was in need of a partial liver transplant that the State of California denied, even though there were donor matches in his family who offered to help. This blatant denial of medical care was, we believed, to be in direct response to his refusal to do what the parole board ordered. Eventually he was transferred to a medical facility, where he died. He'd been sentenced to life with possibility of parole, not death. Though I disliked many of his ways, I did enjoy speaking to him about motorcycles and going on bike runs. In prison, he had the respect of some and was feared by many.

Finally in August 2011, after years of trying to get information from Immigration Customs Enforcement, they finally sent me some documents. The first was Dr Wetmore's affidavit. Along with it came copies of the letter that had accompanied me from the Isle of Man and a letter to Immigration Customs Enforcement, responding to a request from the orphanage in Canada I'd been sent to.

It took me three tries to read Dr Wetmore's affidavit as I found myself getting increasingly angry, knowing that he knew so much about my family and history and had kept it from me. It spoke of him financially helping my first wife get her divorce on the promise that she kept my oldest son from me. I read that he'd actually arranged the "accidental" meeting when I met Tricia in 1982, and that he'd paid her and Stanley John Kearns to come to Fresno to "do me harm". Even my wife, Amy, was paid to give him information about my activities. It also verified all the information my pen pal had found out about my mother Moya. He knew that Martha, who wasn't my mother so had no legal right to sell me to him, had taken me first to Canada, then brought me into the US – and my paternal grandmother had arranged it all.

Dr Wetmore admitted he also paid Stanley John Kearns (who he stated had a shady look about him) and Martha Kearns, who'd pretended to be my mother and had been married to Stanley's brother, to take the child, John Raymond (Frey) Wetmore away – supposedly back from where he came. The only flaw was that Immigration Customs Enforcement told me no trace of him had ever been found.

In September 2012, I received the best thing I could have

hoped for – a notarised copy of my baptism certificate (a copy of the certified one from Fresno County Superior Court that Dr Wetmore had sent them). It was at least proof I had been born and baptised in the Isle of Man. I was British by birth. With the information my pen pal had found, my mother's side went back to at least 1670 in Birmingham. I had roots that couldn't be denied, but we still had to get the British authorities to recognise me and help get me home.

My pen pal and the staff at Prisoners Abroad continued to champion my cause, even enlisting a genealogist on the Isle of Man. Additionally she contacted my defence attorney from my original trial, who was quite surprised I was still in prison. She admitted she'd given my baptism certificate to a person from the British Consulate, though she'd been given orders not to tell them about me. The last part was something else Dr Wetmore had admitted – that he suggested not telling the consulate, so it wouldn't raise international interest in my case, as he realised it would be his undoing.

Due to some court challenges over lengthy denials being given out, I was able to be placed on the 2013 calendar for a hearing. In June 2013, I appeared for the fifth time before a parole board. The commissioner and deputy commissioner had actually read through my file in a meticulous manner.

"Mr Kane, your life reads like a Victorian novel," said the commissioner during the decision part of the hearing. "I would suggest if you ever get out that you write a book. This panel finds you 'Suitable for Parole'." He pointed out that it would have to go before the Governor – though he was letting people go home, he did deny some.

Now I was a lifer with a date, who had to wait for up to 150 days to see if I would actual get out and be deported.

On day 148, the Governor denied my release, which meant I would have to go back to board in three years. With hope dashed yet again, I tried to get my pen pal to stop writing, as I knew this decision would hurt her. I'd sent her copies of every board hearing, programme I took and all my "atta boy" chronos, so she could see that I was doing all that was asked.

I just kept my head down working in the mental health department, with the full belief that if I could keep just one guy from joining a gang or coming back to prison, especially with a life sentence, I would have accomplished something – even if I was forced to live out the rest of my life in prison. I would constantly talk to the guys who came in to the clinic. I encouraged, advised and sometimes just listened, but they knew I was there for them. It cost me nothing to try and be a better, more caring person, so I did what I could.

Over the next couple of years, the harassment continued, though I'd started finding more staff to read Dr Wetmore's affidavit, and I made copies for the psychologists I worked for. Everyone who read it couldn't believe the arrogant and self-righteous way Dr Wetmore tried to portray himself. All the psychologists said he was a psychopath and should never have been allowed around children.

Suddenly I had staff members in the mailroom speaking to me. Office workers, and even some guards who'd never written a laudatory chrono in their 20 to 30-year careers, suddenly volunteered to write ones for me. I found out through one of the psychologists that my old boss who'd gone to work in Inmate Records had read things in the confidential section of my C-File that showed I'd been forced to plead guilty to crimes I didn't commit to save my wife's life. So she'd been encouraging other staff she knew to come see for themselves.

In 2014, Immigration Customs Enforcement provided me with yet another document that filled in a piece of the puzzle called my life. This was a letter sent to Dr Wetmore in response to one of his. This letter had been written by my grandmother in the Isle of Man, back in 1971. In it, she acknowledged I was her grandson, and that I'd been sent away to ease a family scandal. This I knew from Dr Wetmore's affidavit, as he'd pointed out my parents had been married in the Catholic Church (even though my mother was Church of England), yet my father chose a civil divorce rather than ask for the Church's permission. Now today that may not seem like much, but in the 1950s to a devout Catholic family it was a scandal of great magnitude.

Finally in 2016, I was going back to the parole board for the sixth time. I figured since nothing had changed since my last hearing in 2013, other than I'd done more time inside, more programmes completed and accrued more "good" time credits, I would be found suitable again. Besides, I'd received a "status letter" from the British Secretary of State, acknowledging I was a British citizen, born in 1954 in the Isle of Man. The only thing it didn't say was that I'd been stolen and sold. Instead, it went with the more politically correct term "unofficial adoption", when speaking of Dr Wetmore's possession of me. In August 2016, the British Consulate had raised the question to the US Government, about why, if they knew in 1983 I was a British citizen, the consulate hadn't been informed.

This parole hearing was by far the worst one I'd ever attended. The commissioner started off with the fact she'd been married to a Vietnam vet who suffered with post-traumatic stress disorder (PTSD), so knew all about us. Usually you don't know anything about the board member's lives, but this one shared a lot, way too much, and neither the deputy commissioner nor my attorney said anything to her about it. The hearing was mainly focused on her life, her feelings and how men, especially Vietnam vets, were scum. To say she had issues would have been an understatement. Yet after the longest four hours of my life, she finally calmed down enough to give me a three-year denial, which my attorney felt was quite good considering how the hearing went. That really was the attitude of most of the attorneys who represented lifers. To them, it was trying to get the lowest number of years in denial that counted, not getting a parole date, and quite honestly when a parole date was given they were often more surprised than the inmate.

The only good thing resulting from this hearing was that my attorney was able to grab a couple of documents I'd never seen before. The first was a copy of my parole officer's report, the document that every parole board looks at, and believes, before a hearing. It was eleven pages long – eight pages longer than the parole officer's report I'd been given and, when examined, was found to contain over 20 probable lies about my past. The other was a copy of my plea hearing, which I had been told by the court I couldn't have as it had been destroyed. It contained information that proved that everyone in the courtroom back in 1984, apart from me, knew I hadn't been officially adopted by Dr Wetmore, and was therefore an illegal alien, and they were also aware that the British Consulate hadn't been informed.

Because of the erratic behaviour of my commissioner at the hearing, I was able to apply for and get granted an advance hearing the following year. Everyone I spoke to said the same thing – that for certain the next board would find me suitable again.

I received word in March 2017 that my British passport

had been issued and my pen pal held it for when I needed it. That was such a relief. I figured having that extra bit of information to take with me to my next parole hearing could only help my situation. I was ready this time – I knew I was going home. My celly had moved into a single man cell about a month earlier, but as he was just across the tier I was able to quickly share the news with him. After all we'd been cellies for longer than both my marriages together had lasted and he'd tried to help, by doing appeals for board denials, though we were never successful in the courts. He truly believed this would be a game changer for me.

Now it was August 2017 and I was going before my seventh parole board. My attorney was yet another state-appointed one. When he asked if I was ready. I asked who the board members were. A strange look came over his face, and he said the same ones as last hearing. I'm sure he saw the look in my eyes, because he said it couldn't be as bad as last time. I immediately decided I wouldn't go in that room and be berated for another three to four hours by the commissioner with all her problems. My pen pal and I had discussed that if this were to happen, I would postpone and wait for a different board.

Seeing I wasn't happy about the situation and realising I was about to get up and leave, my attorney grabbed my arm.

"You know board members can be one way on a particular day and completely different the next," he said. "I really think you need to go in to this hearing."

Something in his voice, more than his words, made me decide to take a chance. So into the Dragon's Den I went. To my surprise, the commissioner smiled and was more than courteous in her opening remarks. For the next two-and-a-half hours, she never raised her voice. I gave very short answers to questions from her, the deputy commissioner, the District Attorney or my attorney. The whole thing played out almost like an episode of the Twilight Zone, as it was the far opposite of my last hearing with her.

While I waited in the holding cell for them to deliberate on their decision, my attorney came to see me.

"See it wasn't as bad this time," he said.

I had to agree with him, though I told him I still felt she was about to do me, by giving me a longer denial than the last one.

Finally the guard came to take me back into the board-room, I tried to get a read on the room, but nothing gave anything away. The District Attorney was smiling, my attorney wasn't and none of the board members showed anything but poker faces. Then the commissioner looked up from her stack of papers.

"Mr Kane, we have had a very productive hearing today and I would personally like to thank you for attending," she said in an almost-eerie tone. "The panel has decided to find you suitable for parole."

Did she just say I was being found "suitable" – this same

woman who last year yelled at me?

I then heard her say those famous words. "This decision is still up for review by the state governor to confirm and, if he does, it is noted you will be turned over to Immigration and Customs Enforcement for Deportation back to the UK. This hearing is closed and we wish you well."

I was in shock as I walked back to my housing unit, still not sure it had happened. Yet as I went down the corridor, staff members congratulated me. It was the policy that when a lifer had gone to board, whatever the decision the guard working the board area would notify the watch office as well as the unit. So it seemed like everyone knew, because as I walked by the library windows inmates inside gave me a thumbs up. The reception in the unit was much the same, and the Paisas seemed to be some of those who were the happiest for me.

Now the wait was on. I'd always told guys that the 150-day wait was harder and longer in many ways than the years getting the parole date. On 18 December, after 138 days, the word came I would be going to Immigration Customs Enforcement the next day. I was picked up from Deuel Vocational Institution at 6:30 am on 19 December 2017. I was now out of state custody and in federal custody, but I knew now I would be seeing the UK.

I was going home and my life would start again.

25

Immigration Customs Enforcement (ICE) Detention

Driving out of Deuel Vocational Institution, a wave of relief came over me. Even though I knew I wasn't quite free, I was closer to it than I had been in 34 years. No matter how bad things got or how hopeless they seemed, the one thing I hadn't let happen was to allow the system to win. Now I was proving it hadn't.

The Immigration Customs Enforcement agent drove me to their office in Stockton, where after an hour or so they put me back in the van. We drove to their head office in Sacramento. There, I was finally let out of the leg chains and handcuffs and placed in a dirty and cramped holding cell with about a dozen other guys, some of whom were trying to sleep on the floor. Almost two hours later, an agent handed us all brochures about ICE detention centres and what we could expect there. The photos made them look like a college campus and showed lots of people who all seemed happy to be there. Somehow, I knew that this wasn't what they would be like.

Sure enough, a couple of hours later, I was taken from the cell along with three Paisas, and we were shackled and ushered into a van. It was a fairly short ride into the rural area outside Sacramento and we pulled up to the Rio Cosumnes Correctional Center, an overflow facility for the county jail. We found out that ICE rented a couple of wings here for detainees, which is what we were now called – we were no longer prisoners, but detainees. I personally couldn't see the difference – we were still handcuffed and chained and we were still locked up.

We were placed in a wing with about 200 other guys – some had been in detention for as long as two years. Most were fighting deportation, whereas I was looking forward to it. I had told every ICE agent I could that I would sign anything that helped me leave America. However, as I waited with these men, I learned that for many of them, especially those from Mexico, Central America and the Middle East, going back to where they came from would most likely mean death. Some had escaped war, some from drug cartels and all from poverty; most of them had family in America, including children who themselves were American citizens.

After about two weeks of sitting there and getting no answers, I was getting bored. Then I noticed one young guy from Honduras struggling to fill out a 20-page document, so I asked if I could help. At first he seemed hesitant, but then he explained it was his application for asylum form the ICE agent had given him. He had to fill it out and send it to the court, but he couldn't read English very well and didn't understand what to do with it. It took me a few minutes to read through it and realise that these applications were bullshit – that they were meant to keep these guys from being able to easily fill them out.

Now I had a mission: I told anyone who wanted help filling out their applications for asylum that I would do it for them. Besides, the only other things to do there were sleep or watch TV. Within a month, I had filled out and filed 46 applications, of which 22 were granted by the courts. It was shortly after the fifteenth or sixteenth one that I was visited by two ICE agents.

"Why are you helping these people stay in America?" they asked me.

"It's not my country so if I can help them with their dreams and keep families together I will," I replied.

"In the last three years, only a dozen or so applications for asylum have been filed and none has been granted." They were clearly upset. "Yet here you are, not only filling out a lot more but so far all the ones you've done have been granted."

When they told me to stop, I said I would if they sent me home. When I called the consulate later that day, they told me they'd received complaints that I was helping the guys in the detention centre to apply for asylum. They also told me I should stop to avoid upsetting the Americans.

"Well they've upset me for my entire life," I replied. "If they want me to stop, they should just send me home."

Just two days later, at 3am, I was woken by a call over the loud speaker saying I was being deported in just an hour's time. After saying goodbye to all the guys there and wishing them all the best, I was shackled up for a final time and transported to Sacramento Airport, where I was met by two ICE agents who would accompany me back to the UK. We flew from Sacramento in California to Atlanta in Georgia, where we had a four-hour layover before getting on a flight to London. In Atlanta, we were joined by an air marshal, who sat behind me and made the threat that if I "acted squirrelly" he would shoot me.

I remained cuffed until we arrived at Heathrow. We'd been the first to board the plane, but were the last to depart. As we got to the door, the pilot stopped us and said to the ICE agents, "Don't let the British authorities see him in restraints – they won't like it." So with great reluctance, they removed the cuffs.

With an ICE agent tightly gripping each of my arms and the air marshal directly behind me, we proceeded to customs. We came across a nice lady who looked at my passport for a moment and then said to me with a smile, "Welcome home." She said she would get an immigration officer and, within moments came back with a man in a suit, carrying a locked box. Once she'd opened the box, she turned to the air marshall and told him to place his gun and magazine in it. You could see he wasn't happy. When he said he would be flying back out the following day, she responded, "You can have it back then." After he'd complied with her request, she locked the box and gave him a piece of paper with a number on it before walking away with the box.

The immigration official looked at my passport. "How long have you been away from the UK?" he asked.

"Sixty-three years."

"So why have you come back?"

"Because it's home."

"Welcome home," he said with a big smile, and pointed me to the luggage carousel and told me how to get out of Heathrow.

Thanking him, I turned to leave. As I walked away, one of the ICE agents told the immigration official that I had just been deported.

"That may be true, but he's home now and a free man," the official replied.

It was 13 February 2018.

"Free man" – never were two words sweeter to hear. I took what felt like the longest walk ever, as I tried to find my way out of Heathrow and on to the Tube, which I'd never ridden on before. Then, to my delight, I saw my pen pal, standing just as she said she would in her bright red anorak and waving at me. With the biggest hug I'd felt in years, she grabbed my arm and led me down the escalator onto the Picadilly line. The ride was surreal and she was worried about how I'd react to being underground, but all was fine. She took me back to her house, which was one of the most welcoming feelings I'd ever experienced.

The following day, I went to the offices of Prisoners Abroad to meet my case worker and thank everyone there for their support. I'd been a client for 17 years – longer than anyone else in the organisation's history. Even today, over a year later, I still drop off language books and clothing to them, helping the next person who's locked up overseas or has just arrived home in the UK.

I'll end my story there but have two questions:

1. What really happened to the original John Raymond (Frey) Wetmore, the child I replaced after he was "taken away" by Stanley John Kearns, as directed by Dr Charles Henry Wetmore?

2. Who really had a motive to kill Stanley John Kearns?

    (a) Dr Charles Henry Wetmore, who was concerned by what Kearns knew about the disappearance of the original John Raymond Wetmore and was in a position to plea bargain his way out of the charges he was facing?

(b) despite never being charged by the police over the murder, Tricia Kearns, who had Stanley Kearns arrested and had accused him of trying to murder her son, had forged checks on his account, provided my wife with the medication capsules that were subsequently doctored with poison, and who was the sole beneficiary after his death?

I leave those thoughts for you to ponder...

AFTERWORD

I have been home for almost 18 months, and it has been very comforting to have met people who have embraced me, as friends and in some cases even family. However the fact that I never got to know my real family as they have all long passed away, it has become a mission to learn all I can about them. I have visited the flat my father lived in for more than 25 years in Edmonton, and soon I will go to the Remembrance Garden where my Mother's ashes were left, then I hope to go to the Isle of Man to see where I was born and in Birmingham visit all the places my family lived and enjoyed. None of this will change the past, though for me it will allow me hopefully a bit of insight into those people from whom I come from. I truly believe that much of the strength I have had throughout my life came not from me, but from those who came before me.

As for the future, who can say what it may hold? I would like to get back to working on motorcycles, a great love I have had since I was a child and of course coming from the

Isle of Man, it may have instilled in my spirit. I certainly am planning to give back to the community in the way of volunteering, as I feel it is very important that to be a part of a community, a person must play a part in that community. So I am hoping to be able to get involved in helping our youths to avoid getting caught up in gangs and going down the wrong path.

My past will never leave me, but I will not allow it to define me or bind me from having a bright and happy future and I certainly wish that for every one – to find what makes them happy and embrace it to the fullest.

Just remember to always "Hold Your Mud", as you are special and important to others.

Cheers, Jamie Morgan Kane

ACKNOWLEDGEMENTS

I truly believe that the charity Prisoners Abroad played a big part in helping me get through a lot of frustrating times. I was a client of theirs for about 17 years (half my prison term) and they were always there to answer my question and raise my spirits. So I thank the whole team, as many worked on my situation while I was in prison, helping with my resettlement.

However, I would be remiss not to thank some of the staff and inmates who also believed in me and provided encouragement over the years. So this is a thank you, though I could never name everyone, to AW, C/O's M & M, Dr K, Dr P and those who I did years with and some who are still in – Jason, Jose, Rusty, Tom, Dan, Latyiff and Jamal. My best to each and every one of you.

Thanks also to the Mirror Books team: Ajda, Julie, George, Paula, Danny, Charlotte, Jo and Melanie. I couldn't have done this without you.